110.

David with much love from
Mum.
        Christmas 1970
        Birthday   71.

Separate Horizons

The Reverend
STEPHEN PAKENHAM

Separate Horizons

a definitive survey
of the Singlehanded Transatlantic Race

Adlard Coles
Erroll Bruce
Richard Creagh-Osborne

Nautical House
Lymington, Hampshire

Nautical Publishing Company

in association with George G. Harrap & Co. Ltd.,
London, Toronto, Sydney, Wellington

SBN 245 59678 X

First published in Great Britain by
NAUTICAL PUBLISHING COMPANY
Nautical House, Lymington, Hampshire

Composed in 11 on 12 pt Monotype Baskerville
and made and printed in Great Britain by
Compton Press, Compton Chamberlayne,
Salisbury, Wiltshire

for
ELIZABETH
who
helped me to go
inspired my return
and then
prompted & supported the writing

Contents

Plates

The Sea   *by John Laurent Giles*

What is this sea — this dour and lovely mistress of
                                     most cherished woes?
What is this wind, this harsh impeller of enthralled souls?
What are these waves, this sky these clouds,
                         the welcome sunshine and the distant shore?
That is no water — that no moving stream of air!
Those are no undulations on the surface formed
   to trochoids by the rolling particles within!
No boundless space–no water vapour those–
   no waves of light and heat of length and speed precisely known!
No rock, no sand and clay in random quantities
   admixed with vegetation clothed that land informs!

This is the sea, this joy of life apart,
   this thrill of challenge to the might of Nature.
This is the wind, this fickle goddess of tempestuous smiles;
These are the waves whose dormant or uplifted wrath
   calms or inspires our inmost fears.
This is the sky, this blue–how blue!–the overarching
                                     canopy of earth
set with the billowing white, the fleecy or the
                                     thunderous clouds of storm.
This is the sunshine warming our hearts, our eyes regaling with
   the azure blues and greens struck glinting from the waves.
This is the distant land, this blue of hills, this green atop of black
and rocky cliff, this splash of surf so white about its foot.
This is the ship that lifts our hearts to heaven,
                     the hard, unchanging line and colour of the hull,
                         the rythmic masts and wind-pressed sails above.
The sailor ne'er accounts his life but dreams; how else could he
   the torment of the storm survive, to turn once more at voyage
                                     end
   and trace again his steps in reeling hulls

that sicken, maim or soak his body in the clutching sea?
His body is but meat and bones and blood driven to labour
                                              by the soul within;
   it is not suited to the sea save by a fleeting effort of the will.
But to his soul to ride upon those waves,
   to bend those winds to his advantage and to move
   in some direction that he wills — to pass triumphant
                                              on that fickle sea,
   that is the glory of the ocean's call.
So to his ship his soul is bound; no ties of earth can make him
   slave to spend his life at sea, but wild
   romance the mental bonds of fate.
This is the joy which takes him forth again, despite
                                              his body's plaints;
   this great adventure, this plying of the deep, this sea,
   this wind, these waves, this sky, these clouds, this
                                              sunshine and the shore.
These compound the nectar for his soul
   which feeds on beauty and on God.

                              John Laurent Giles

Author's note

Before I began this book, I asked a considerable variety of people how they would like the race explained. Almost invariably, men wanted the technical answers on navigation, relative positions of the boats, types of rig, equipment, gear failure etc. By contrast, women were interested in how we felt; they wanted an honest picture of our emotions, of how well we slept and fed; when did grey days look black, and blue ones seem golden!

For fifteen months I gathered as much information as I could from those who sailed in the race, trying to let the facts themselves make the overall picture; details which at first seemed irrelevant often became significant in the final analysis. The story then incorporated directly perhaps a fifteenth part of the research material.

In the chartwork, the only positions I have used for boats have been those given to me, and the aim in accuracy has been to plot them to the nearest mile and keep them so through each stage of reproduction. It would have been convenient for clarity to calculate likely midday positions to replace those given at other times of the day; this would have produced a nice uniformity in the chartwork, but I have resisted the temptation as it would have been mis-handling on my part!

Various times were being kept during the race, e.g. G.M.T. throughout, and I have altered these so that the comparisons of both incidents and positions can be in zone or local time.

No one can say how near the chart positions are to the true positions of the boats! What one can say is that those sailing south by way of the Azores should have been able to quote chart positions within a few miles of their true positions: the sun was normally shining on a clear horizon–ideal for sunsights–and the southern boats were not so buffetted as those to the north where less accurate navigation had to be expected; it is not easy to take a swift sunsight on a glimpse of the sun, from a jerking boat, peering at a doubtful horizon.

The point to emphasise is this: my analysis is of *chart* positions; I am not pretending to give *true* positions, and the distinction should be kept in mind.

Straight lines have normally been drawn between positions as is the custom for this type of analysis; the boats were, of course, often weaving to the wind between the positions, particularly those to the north.

*   *   *

This book could not have been produced without the admirable and generous co-operation of those who sailed with me in the race; the substance of the story bears out the high degree of their help.

Among the many others who have patiently answered my questions I wish to thank especially Terence Shaw and Jack Odling-Smee of the Royal Western Yacht Club for their help with background material, as also the staff of *The Observer;* Robert Clark for imparting wisdom on yachts in general and on his in particular; Ian Slater for a great deal of information on the computer which advised Geoffrey Williams; also Vic Farrant for lending his ability to read French fluently.

As work had to start with a rush in Newport, Rhode Island, I warmly thank Arthur Newell for lending me his car, and his wife Mary for constantly feeding me; The Reverend John Turnbull for lending me the top floor of his Rectory (space was somewhat limited at the end when a pop group moved in!); I also thank Bill Thomas, Pete Dunning, Dr Robin Wallace, Robert Quarry, Jim and Jeane Hayman, John Mathinos, Jay Lemaire, Tom and Evelyn Lenthall — I cherish the happiest of memories of my ten days in Newport.

I am very grateful to Noel Bevan for giving the description of his electronics on board *Myth of Malham*, and Commander Vanrenen for supplying information on the Gulf Stream.

My grateful thanks are also due to the following for permission to quote: the Secretary of the Royal Naval Sailing Association — an article by Leslie Williams published in the Association's Journal; Michael Richey — his article published in the *Journal of the Institute of Navigation;* Count Bertrand de Castelbajac — the dedication in his book on the race, *de Plymouth à Newport;* also the Editor of the *Yachting World* for the description of *Sir Thomas Lipton* published in August 1968, and further the Director General of The Meteorological Office for permission to trace the information provided in the weather charts for 8th–15th June 1968.

I wish to thank *The Observer* for giving permission to use the pictures taken by Chris Smith, and also Corrall Print for the photograph entitled "Transatlantic Incident." I am very grateful also for the photographs given by Noel Bevan and Eric Willis.

Among those who have helped with the preparation of the book for the publisher, a special mention is due to Pamela Bartlett for her care and artistry in the chartwork, and to John Sharp for his beautiful miniatures of the boats.

It added fine treasure to this book when the late Jack Giles offered for inclusion his poem; I will always be deeply grateful for the wise support he gave to my sailing and writing.

I owe a great debt to Pauline Dunster who read through the typescript at two stages and punctured my pride with penetrating suggestions for improvements. (How amazing that we were still good friends at the end!)

The greatest debt I owe is to my wife who typed the book not only twice but many times through in parts, having first handled the enormous volume of research material. She has helped in many other ways; in particular she chose and gathered the photographs — I applaud her choice for its variety and interest.

So many other people remain unmentioned who have helped to produce this book; my sincere gratitude is due to all of them; especially to my wife, my fellow-competitors and Pauline Dunster — how much they have achieved can be understood when I say that two years ago I no more considered myself capable of completing a book than of conducting an orchestra!

Five boats sailed from Plymouth on Saturday 11th June 1960 in the first singlehanded Transatlantic Race. Sir Francis Chichester's Gipsy Moth III, *the largest boat with an overall length of 39 feet, won in 40 days.*

The race was conceived by Colonel Hasler; it is sponsored by The Observer *and organised by the Royal Western Yacht Club of England.*

In the second race in 1964, 15 boats took part, the biggest being Eric Tarbarly's Pen Duick II, *44 feet overall, which won in 27 days.*

The third race started at 1100 on Saturday 1st June 1968 and again Eric Tarbarly had the largest yacht, Pen Duick IV, *66 feet overall.*

1 Plymouth Sound

We had not dared to discuss how we would say goodbye; now, in the quiet drizzle, it would be upon us immediately the launch came alongside.

If only I could have gallantly produced a bunch of flowers from behind my back. Ridiculous idea! There had been no opportunity in the last day to buy them unobserved, let alone hide them on board. That apart, I had no right to attempt the gallant poise; my mind raced back over three years of preparation for the race — Elizabeth had worked like a slave to help me go away on my own.

Together we had set the sails to take *Rob Roy* across the starting line, and while identifying the yachts around us I suddenly realised that Elizabeth could no longer share our boat with me — we waved to the naval launch which had towed us out. We watched it approaching, hardly seeming man and wife as we stood in silence, separated by our cold and dripping oilskins. Then wet orange arms gripped wet orange coats, a damp mouth pressed against a cool cheek, and I heard myself murmuring, "Thank you, darling, for everything". Elizabeth jumped to the launch and other arms gathered her in.

That was it, just "thank you for everything" after eleven years happily shared in four homes and two boats filled with the noise and toys of three children. *Rob Roy* and I were suddenly separated from all that was family and home.

I tried to concentrate on the race — the wind had failed in the drizzle and I could not reach the starting line before the gun. This meant that I had to use the oars, a magnificent pair designed and made by a kind friend. Like so much of the gear, they had come on board at the last moment, and with little time for trying them out, I felt nervous at the prospect of using them now before such a crowd of onlookers.

When the heavy outriggers were screwed in position, the life-raft was unlashed and pushed forward out of the way. Then the oars–15 feet long–were unstrapped from their stowage in the cabin, eased out over the stern and forward again into the outriggers.

After several minutes it dawned on me that I had crossed the starting line rowing, and suddenly I felt gay. I rowed ahead to a group of boats in the race and started chatting to fellow-competitors. The gentle rain had quietly closed us in on each other and we could ignore the thronging spectator boats. By convention it should have been a grand occasion, hectic and festive, the boats fluttering out their burgees proudly while tacking to a brisk headwind — for the spectators the exciting chance of a resounding collision.

I pushed my way slowly past Noel Bevan in *Myth of Malham*. "Sorry to do this on you," I said — "I did just want to be able to say that I was ahead of you at one point in the race!" Somewhat tensely, Noel tended the sheet of his ghosting genoa to coax more air along the sail; then he relaxed with a broad grin and answered the quip — he knew he would soon show me a clean pair of heels.

Next ahead was Bruce Dalling aboard *Voortrekker*, sitting comfortably in his cockpit — an even cleaner pair of heels there. We bantered easily, until suddenly he produced a coil of rope and said, "Hi Rev! Wait a minute . . . "

A light air filled our sails; I trailed the oars while trimming my sheets — Noel and Bruce came up swiftly. Then the bright yellow proa, *Cheers*, appeared as though from nowhere. Tom Follett was sitting on top–there was little room inside his boat– completely relaxed like a benign Buddha. "Hope you have a pleasant trip," he drawled with American courtesy. The gentle wind faded, but Tom glided on. Very eerie — I half expected him to turn round and raise a hand in blessing.

The brief wind brought a distinguished boat close to our group — the long, low and beautifully sleek *Sir Thomas Lipton*, unmistakeable with her blue masts. But something was wrong. The newcomer was silent. We were ignored by Geoffrey

Williams who went forward to busy himself in a pile of head-sails. I felt embarrased; should one have tried to break through the wall which Geoffrey seemed to have built around himself? Alone among the yachts assembling for the race, his had not followed the general instruction to enter Millbay Dock, and the Race Committee had imposed a 12-hour penalty on him.

Another stir of wind — *Myth of Malham* and *Rob Roy* began to converge. Technically this was interesting: if I was rowing, Noel had right of way. As I pushed hard on one oar to avoid him it seemed that one or both of us might hit *Sir Thomas Lipton*. Even these antics were ignored by Geoffrey Williams.

The spectator boats crowding the sides of our cleared channel thinned out past the breakwater, but we hardly noticed them as we concentrated on each other in the fitful wind.

Then a familiar launch came close aboard. "Well done, darling, you have rowed into sixth place." After snippets of news about other boats, an awkward pause — "We have got to go back now."

Her eyes were sparkling moistly as she looked at me; was she accusing me for sailing away on my own, or was I accusing myself? In fact she was wondering if she would ever see me again.

We looked at each other across the water with a simple longing as the launch turned and gathered speed for Plymouth. I attended to something or other on board and when I looked back I could not see her.

I searched and searched for one last glimpse; half of my life had left me. The Plymouth landmarks and surrounding headlands were fading white in the mist.

Ahead the sun was shining softly on a haze mantled across the bay — lazily, the race had started.

Race No.	Yacht	Crew	Nationality	Rig	Overall length in feet
1	Pen Duick IV*	Eric Tabarly	French	Ketch (Tri)	66
42	Raph*	Alain Gliksman	French	Ketch	58
44	Sir Thomas Lipton	Geoffrey Williams	British	Ketch	56.2
9	Spirit of Cutty Sark	Leslie Williams	British	Sloop	53.2
12	San Giorgio*	Alex Carozzo	Italian	Ketch (Cat)	53
2	Voortrekker	Bruce Dalling	South African	Ketch	50
8	Coila*	Eric Willis	British	Ketch (Tri)	50
43	Yaksha*	Joan de Kat	French	Sloop (Tri)	50
35	Ocean Highlander	Sandy Munro	British	Cutter (Cat)	45
13	Golden Cockerel	Bill Howell	Australian	Ketch (Cat)	43
33	Gancia Girl	Martin Minter-Kemp	British	Ketch (Tri)	42
34	Guntur III*	Guy Piazzini	Swiss	Ketch	41
41	Cheers	Tom Follett	U.S.A.	Schooner (Proa)	40
6	Myth of Malham	Noel Bevan	British	Cutter	39.7
23	Zeevalk*	Robert Wingate	British	Sloop	39.6
21	Koala III*	Edith Baumann	German	Sloop (Tri)	39.4
38	Mex	Claus Hehner	German	Sloop	37
47	Ambrima*	Marco Cuiklinski	French	Sloop	37
37	Sylvia II	André Foëzon	French	Sloop	36
40	La Delirante*	Lionel Paillard	French	Sloop	36
45	Maguelonne	Jean Yves Terlain	French	Sloop	35
39	Maxine	Bertrand de Castelbajac	French	Sloop	34.8
25	White Ghost*	Michael Pulsford	British	Schooner (Tri)	34
30	Startled Faun	Colin Forbes	British	Sloop (Tri)	33
32	Aye-Aye*	Egon Hienemann	German	Sloop	33
7	Rob Roy	Stephen Pakenham	British	Ketch	32.4
14	Opus	Brian Cooke	British	Sloop	32
31	Dogwatch	Nigel Burgess	British	Sloop	27.8
17	Wileca*	William Wallin	Swedish	Sloop	27
16	Atlantis III*	David Pyle	British	Ketch	26.5
20	Tamouré*	Bernard Waquet	French	Sloop (Tri)	26.3
27	Jester	Michael Richey	British	Chinese Lug	25.9
19	Amistad	Bernard Rodriquez	U.S.A.	Cutter (Tri)	25
24	Fione	Bertil Enbom	Swedish	Sloop	19.7
3	Goodwin II	Åke Mattsson	Swedish	Sloop	19·7

*Retired

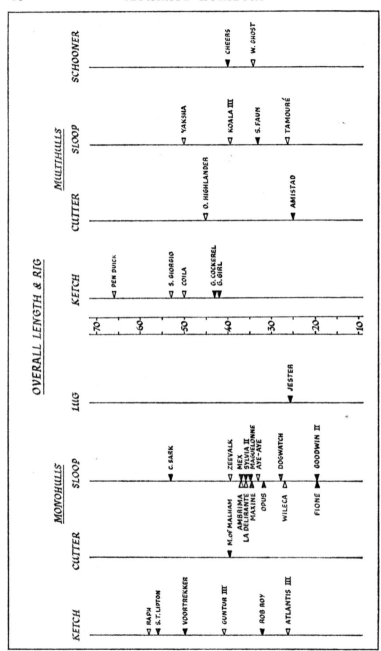

2 Softly through the bay   *1 June*

Away on his own, Eric Tabarly stood out into the bay. He was favourite to win by the betting odds at Ladbrookes — with good reason. He had won the 1964 race by the convincing margin of 2 days 20 hours (perhaps it was inevitable as de Gaulle had kissed him on both cheeks). This win became the pride of France; Eric was seconded from the Navy to the French Ministry of Sport to be devoted whole time to his sailing.

His ideas for the 1968 race had first developed into a schooner which for a season dominated the racing in the English Channel. The Royal Ocean Racing Club has reason to remember 1967 as the year of *Pen Duick III;* but by the end of her first season Eric considered her obsolete for the 1968 singlehanded race. He had been deeply impressed by a fast sail along the Channel in the trimaran *Toria,* winner of the 1966 Round Britain Race, and Eric decided to have a similar but much larger trimaran for himself.

So came the ketch *Pen Duick IV* — her plans and construction were rushed through during the winter before the race. She was longer than *Toria* by more than 50 per cent, but although in theory she should crush the opposition, her design raised practical problems: how easily could a boat covering nearly the area of a tennis court be sailed through an Atlantic gale? The designer had clearly met problems in calculating the likely strains, but the essential trials at sea did not take place because strikes in France delayed the launching until a bare fortnight before the race.

Toria was herself in the race — renamed *Gancia Girl.* Martin Minter-Kemp, who had been crew for her designer, Derek Kelsall, in the Round Britain Race, was now in command. He has described *Gancia Girl* as "the first of a new generation

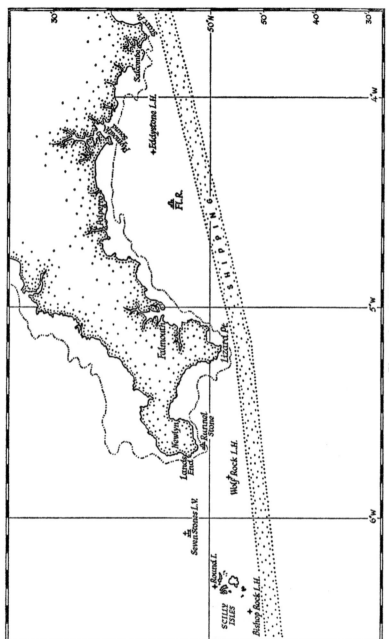

Plymouth to Scillies

of high aspect trimarans: that is to say, the wing floats are mounted high relative to the centre hull. This means that in her normal attitude the weather float flies clear of the water, reducing the wetted area and, in theory, making her more manoeuvrable as well as faster."

Her rig was changed for the race from sloop to staysail ketch, converting two large sails into four smaller ones — a classic example of re-rigging for singlehanding. The smaller mainsail would rarely be reefed — it would normally be right up or right down. Also, with two pairs of forestays, four headsails could be continuously hanked on; when a headsail was lowered it could be left on deck, lashed down, and this arrangement largely avoided the heavy work of changing headsails — much easier to have them, like the mainsail, simply up or down.

Pen Duick IV had a clear lead over one group of boats straggling out towards the open sea; *Spirit of Cutty Sark* led another, tighter, group hugging the coast, hoping that the mist would clear sufficiently for a sea breeze to develop.

For several reasons *Spirit of Cutty Sark* was an interesting entry. Mid-size among the biggest eight boats, alone in that group she was not designed specifically for the race. She was the second to be launched in the 53-foot Gallant class, designed by the famous Dutchman, E. G. Van de Stadt. At the time of the race the Gallants were the largest stock boats built in glass fibre, and with a displacement of 15 tons *Spirit of Cutty Sark* was easily the heaviest boat in the race. The design allowed for various rigs among which the sloop had been deliberately chosen, this in contrast to the smaller *Gancia Girl*, changed from sloop to ketch. The displacement and the rig clearly called for a powerful man, and Leslie Williams had been named "the quiet giant" by the Press. The sails on *Spirit of Cutty Sark* were, in fact, as large as he reckoned he could handle — he said himself that anything larger would have required the rig to be divided into smaller areas. As it was, his largest genoa had an area of 860 square feet — almost four times the size of the mainsail and jib together on *Fione* and *Goodwin II*, the two smallest boats in the race.

It was an incongruously lazy afternoon for starting this supposedly grim ocean race. A spinnaker was hoisted on

Gunthur III; it briefly filled and then collapsed — Guy Piazzini
inadvertantly headed back towards his native Switzerland.
Nearby, *Ocean Highlander* was pointing Sandy Munro eastwards — on a line for Soho!

Bill Howell was heading his catamaran, *Golden Cockerel*,
in pursuit of *Pen Duick IV*. Bill is a dentist, an Australian never
at a loss for a wisecrack. When first he saw *Pen Duick IV* he
surveyed the arching system of aluminium girders joining the
three hulls and then declared that they were sailing Sydney
Bridge into Millbay Dock.

He drifted towards *Voortrekker* and smiled as he watched
Bruce Dalling "changing headsails like mad." Bruce paused
to mutter, "How did that Tabarly get out there?" Bill replied,
"Forget it Bruce–there's another 30 days to go–you are trying
too bloody hard. Get below and have a meal!"

Bill was enjoying a beer. He had to leave it while they
fended each other off; then he said, "Come aboard and have
a look around — you have not seen the boat."

Bill could afford to be relaxed this afternoon — he was one
of the most experienced offshore men in the race having
sailed some 30,000 miles of open sea, including the last race
in 1964. His experience and boisterous personality made him
a natural draw for the Press. He had been reported as taking
disposable paper pants to reduce the washing, but in his
experiments before the race he had simply split them.

Outwardly undaunted by the fact that his 43-foot *Golden
Cockerel* was racing against nine larger boats, his careful sense
of seamanship was epitomised as he headed his logbook
"Plymouth towards Newport" — by convention he should
have written "Plymouth *to* Newport."

Golden Cockerel has the hull of the Imi Loa class designed in
America by Rudy Choy. Normally sloop-rigged for racing,
Rudy Choy had designed a staysail ketch rig for *Golden Cockerel*,
based on a similar design for *World Cat* for her circumnavigation.

Bill set in train what may be called the "booze battle" among
the sponsors, for Courage Ales gave him support in return for
naming his boat *Golden Cockerel*. Cutty Sark Scotch Whisky
entered the lists more thoroughly by providing Leslie Williams
with a Gallant. Watney Mann sponsored Colin Forbes to
produce a film of the race — a wise move as it would be of

lasting value. Gancia Wines helped a renamed *Toria* into the race, while the teetotallers were catered for by Lipton's Tea.

The more massive the sponsoring, the heavier the responsibility — Bruce Dalling carried the greatest weight aboard *Voortrekker*. The South African Ocean Racing Trust had selected him from 40 applicants, the aim of the Trust being to keep international sporting contacts open for South Africa in ocean racing. An enormous number of South Africans were involved in financing *Voortrekker* — some 470,000 *Voortrekker* stamps had been sold at 10 cents each. As he set off, Bruce wrote in his logbook, "All eyes at home are on me and it's a fearful responsibility."

Whereas *Spirit of Cutty Sark* was designed as a stock boat to meet various requirements in racing, cruising and chartering, in the case of *Voortrekker*, Van de Stadt was specifically designing for the race. He concentrated on the lightest displacement possible, keeping the weight down to a mere 6½ tons on a length of 50 feet. (The basic argument towards light displacement is simple: the longer the boat, the faster it can go; the lighter the boat, the smaller the sails needed to drive it — so if a man reckons he can handle 1,000 square feet of sails, then the lighter the hull below those sails, the longer and faster it can be.)

The two largest monohulls–*Raph* and *Sir Thomas Lipton*– sailed beside each other deliberately for several hours during the afternoon. Alain Gliksman–the French half of this *entente cordiale*–is a versatile yachtsman with an impressive racing record; he is editor of *Neptune Nautisme*, a leading French yachting journal. Geoffrey Williams said of the encounter, "we were purposely staying together–for four or five hours– rather enjoying each other's company before the long solo passage." Alain's experienced eye was sizing up the two boats against each other. He found *Sir Thomas Lipton* slightly faster in the light airs–pointing higher into the wind–and easier to handle and tack.

If he did not know the background to *Sir Thomas Lipton*, Alain had rapidly sensed the essential difference between the two boats. *Raph* was designed by André Mauric who enjoys an unrivalled reputation in France; the design, however, required the boat to be a suitable flagship after the race in the new marina at Saint Raphael in the south of France, taking part in conventional crewed racing. Robert Clark, unsurpassed in this country, was given a free hand in designing *Sir Thomas Lipton* with the sole object of one singlehanded win. He drew a low freeboard–restricting accommodation–and achieved a 60 per cent ballast ratio to make the boat very stiff; he then gave much time and thought to the rig, developing ideas for one man to handle large sails at all times without becoming exhausted. Bernard Hayman, who for many years has been editor of *Yachting World*, described *Sir Thomas Lipton* as "one of the loveliest yachts ever built . . . combining sheer beauty with efficiency and superb performance."

Geoffrey Williams must be rated a remarkable competitor to have armed himself with the largest British boat in the race, at the age of 25. He had also developed the novel idea of receiving guidance from a computer in London: each day it would calculate one or more courses for holding good winds and avoiding bad weather — intelligently used, this aid had the potential to gain several days in the race.

Myth of Malham had a light-weight ghoster set which was well suited to the feeble wind, and Noel Bevan enjoyed the afternoon carving his way through the opposition. *Myth of Malham* is the celebrated post-war racing yacht designed by Laurent Giles for Captain John Illingworth; among her many wins were the Fastnet Race in 1947 and 1949. She was considered for the circumnavigation of Sir Alec Rose, but a survey revealed that £2,000 would have to be spent on her. Noel then bought her; he completed the schedule of work in eight week-ends with a number of friends and help from Emsworth Shipyard; this included replacing 300 floor fastenings and 300 garboard fastenings.

Noel is a specialist, a leading expert in microelectronics. Before World War II he was working in the radio industry; during the war he served in the Royal Navy as a telegraphist; after the war he went back for a time to E.M.I., and then in 1950 he joined Elliot Automation where he is Chief Engineer, Naval Division.

The fruits of his specialisation were crammed into *Myth of Malham* with a mass of connecting wires; surely no other racing yacht has put to sea with such a sophisticated array of electronics! (see appendix IV)

Noel was still designing improvements while on passage.

At the moment, however, he was concentrating on the sailing; at 1400 he noted, "Ahead of all except *Spirit of Cutty Sark* and *Yaksha*" — both of these were in the largest group of eight. *Myth of Malham*, 40 feet long, was mid-size in the second group of eight. At 1530 Noel was becalmed for an hour five miles south of Polperro, but by 1800 only *Yaksha* remained ahead.

The trimaran, *Yaksha*, was home-built. As if to compensate for possible weakness, rigging wire was stretched out in every plausible direction, but in Millbay Dock a mast-band had been visibly descending under the strain.

Nevertheless, *Yaksha* was sailing magnificently this afternoon. She was certainly light, and her high aspect sails were making the best of the breeze. We may have laughed at *Yaksha* the boat, but we all liked Joan de Kat the man.

Yaksha was now a mile ahead of *Myth of Malham* and possibly leading the race. At 2000 there was an hour of calm, and then a promising wind arrived from the north-west. At 2115 Noel Bevan had overhauled *Yaksha* and he wrote down triumphantly — "Now ahead of lot!"

A red pin-prick of light appeared for an instant on the port bow; I stood still in the cockpit, concentrating in its direction — at the end of ten seconds it winked again. An unexpected blessing, we had sailed to a buoy anchored more than 12 miles from the shore.

Bill Howell saw it first; at 2100 he passed it some 700 yards on his starboard side. Sandy Munro's course then took him close by. I had the buoy 400 yards to port at 2120.

For several hours the three of us had been engaged in a tussle, of little significance in the race, but certainly of interest in comparing multihulls and monohulls — we were sailing on the starboard tack to a light but steady breeze.

Bill Howell had eased the sheets on his catamaran to edge himself further from the wind — moving at $5\frac{1}{2}$ knots he gradually drew ahead to leeward. In the catamaran *Ocean Highlander*, Sandy Munro was in front of me and to windward, moving steadily under working genoa and mainsail. I had set an extreme ghosting genoa which overlaps the mainmast by nearly 90 per cent; I carefully trimmed the sheets and the vaned steering, and waited to see what would happen between *Ocean Highlander* and *Rob Roy*.

Soon I realised that we were moving at the same speed, a little over $4\frac{1}{2}$ knots. I argued that a monohull in such a light wind could hardly gain significant speed by paying off like Bill Howell (he was continuing to move ahead) — the obvious ploy was to see if I could sail up to windward of Sandy Munro. To my astonishment I sailed from his port quarter to windward on his starboard quarter, maintaining the distance behind him.

Had we been racing to a windward buoy, *Rob Roy* would have arrived first. This may seem remarkable as *Ocean High-*

lander has a 45-foot length against *Rob Roy's* 32, but the tables would undoubtedly be turned with a vengeance in a stronger wind with the sheets freed — there is plenty of 'Box and Cox' when multihulls race against monohulls.

Ocean Highlander, the largest boat in the second group of eight, was aptly called 'the dark horse' of the race. A stock boat of the Ocean Ranger class, she was designed by Roland Prout to be stable, safe and comfortable for cruising; the class, however, shows a bulldog tenacity for holding a good position when racing. Ample accommodation — when Sandy rested he could choose one of 16 bunks!

The warm evening held the sense of balmy unreality of the day. With hardly a ripple to the sea, a milky blue haze was joining ocean and sky as one. The rays of the falling sun were reflecting off the white side and sails of *Golden Cockerel;* she stood out in sharp relief, seeming to glide away over glass.

The breeze dwindled in the fading light. I was musing upon my qualifying cruise two years before; I had stayed at rest one windless night in these same waters, gently rocked in my fitful sleep, watching when awake the winking white light of another vessel also resting some miles away.

The sudden red flash jerked me back to my surroundings. By now the three of us had little idea of our position; the coastline had disappeared hours ago, so the buoy gave us an accurate "departure" (when a ship is set on course for the open sea she is described as "taking departure" from the last position obtained by a fix on the coast, or from passing near an offshore buoy, lighthouse or lightvessel.)

At 2300 Brian Cooke had the same buoy half a mile to port. He describes his 32-foot sloop as "a solid cruising boat, not built for racing at all." Richard Austin had commissioned the lines for the monohull, *Opus,* from Robert Clark; during the eight years it took to build her at his home in Stanmore, Middlesex–assisted by Brian Cooke–there had been no thought of entering her for this race. Indeed, with her solid construction of teak on oak, her high freeboard and low draft, she might be considered unsuitable but for the fact that there were prizes in the race apart from the obvious one for the outright winner: there was one for the fastest monohull on handicap and, further, a silver plate was presented by *The Observer* to each

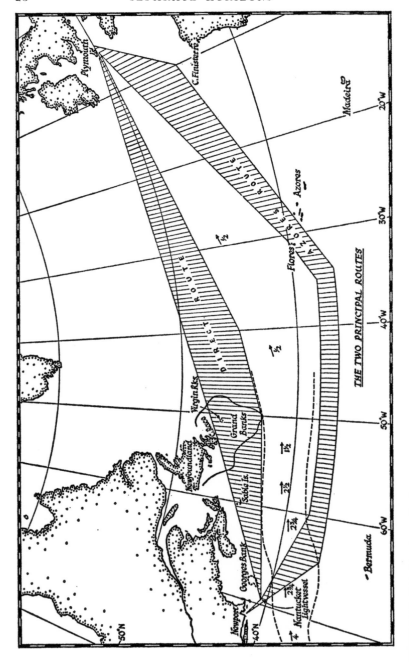

THE TWO PRINCIPAL ROUTES

person who arrived at Newport within two months having obeyed all the rules (e.g., no outside assistance or use of engine).

For Brian Cooke the buoy was not his departure from England — he was making for the Lizard, inside the shipping lane.

Bill Howell and I were crossing the shipping lane as fast as possible to gain the safer water the other side. At 2330 we were among the ships, and an hour later had left them behind. We had lost sight of each other at nightfall, and might not see another yacht until near the American coast.

Tom Follett took departure from the Lizard at 0145. He was moving fast, probably lying second behind *Pen Duick IV*. The first real wind of the day had been freshening from the northwest since 2300; it brought rain and piled up the sea — the honeymoon of the start was abruptly over! Tom was 8 miles from the Lizard, south of the shipping lane. His sheets were freed to reach on a south-west course towards the Azores, although at this stage he had not decided which route to follow.

The two principal routes are shown on the gnomonic chart opposite. The direct route has the Great Circle course as its northern edge, the line of it in fact bent south about 20 miles to round Cape Race, Newfoundland; the southern edge skirts the northern ordinary limit of the Gulf Stream. The first two thirds of this route are sailed against the prevailing winds–frequently strong or gale force–and also against the slow drift of the Atlantic current.

From the Grand Banks onwards one has to expect much fog within which fishing vessels and icebergs are obscured, but one can hope for fitful assistance from the Labrador Current flowing southward round Newfoundland into a general set west-south-west towards Sable Island. This leg from the Banks to Nantucket must also expect frequent calms as well as further head winds; the southern edge of it will reduce the likelihood of fog and icebergs, and increase the chances of better winds, but it will also increase the distance to be sailed.

The direct route is complicated by variations to suit individual tastes; I have therefore drawn it as a broad band across the ocean, opening out from the Scillies and closing again to the Nantucket Lightvessel which is left to starboard before turning northwards for Newport, Rhode Island.

If one wishes to avoid the hazards of taking the shortest way on the direct route, the obvious alternative is to sail southwards by way of the Azores to skirt the southern ordinary limit of the Gulf Stream, heading for what may be a tricky final leg northwards across the Stream. Again, there are variations to this route to suit individual preferences.

The direct route is the more popular of the two despite the fact that it can be wet, cold, dangerous, exhausting, and difficult for navigation; indeed, the boats on the Azores route may even log a shorter total distance if the direct route produces a high proportion of head winds.

During the night of 1st–2nd June, most of the boats sailing by the direct route kept towards the coast to take departure from the Scillies, from Round Island on the northern side or the Bishop Rock Light to the south.

As the wind filled in from north-west, Noel Bevan rapidly lost his lead to the bigger boats behind him; Bruce Dalling apparently passed to the south of him shortly after dark. At 0245 Noel had the Lizard abeam, and he reported his position by Aldis lamp to the coastguard station. At 0315 he saw a yacht $\frac{1}{2}$ mile astern, silhouetted in the beam of the Lizard light; at first he thought it was *Pen Duick IV*, but with daylight it became *Sir Thomas Lipton*. Geoffrey Williams was surprised to find *Myth of Malham* ahead of him, and then took 2 hours to put her hull down. In fact the two boats were diverging, *Sir Thomas Lipton* going north of the Scillies and *Myth of Malham* south. Geoffrey Williams made his departure sailing out between the Seven Stones Lightvessel and Round Island.

At 0600 Noel Bevan had the Wolf Rock abeam. Nigel Burgess, 23 miles behind him, had reached the Lizard. Nigel, Second Officer in the Royal Fleet Auxiliary, was taking the light displacement monohull *Dogwatch* on the Azores route — with a 28 foot length, she was the largest boat in the smallest group of 8. Built in Holland in 1957–one of the first boats made of cold moulded ply–she was designed by U. Van Essen of Flying Dutchman dinghy fame. Although her keel goes down 5 feet, the hull itself sits on top, drawing only 9 inches. Nigel reached the Wolf Rock at 1200, 6 hours after Noel Bevan;

he then left the Bishop Rock Light 5 miles to the north as he was taking the northern edge of the approach route to the Azores, aiming at Corvo, north of Flores.

About 23 miles south of Nigel, and slightly ahead of him, the Chinese lugsail of *Jester* was thrusting Michael Richey on a more southerly approach to the Azores. *Jester* had been sailed in the first two races on a far northerly route unique to Colonel Hasler. The lugsail, similar to those used for centuries on Chinese junks, was Colonel Hasler's answer to the requirements of a simple rig for singlehanding — one unstayed mast supports one solitary sail; the halyards, sheets and reefing lines all lead to one position — no need to balance on a heaving deck for sail changing and reefing. The first race took place in the heyday of the Folkboat, and *Jester* has its standard hull; but there convention ends, for apart from the rig she is decked all over, with a circular control hatch amidships in place of a cockpit aft. This hatch reminds one of the standard British workman's hole — a head pops up at intervals to make sure no intruders are approaching, then down again for a cup of tea (for Michael Richey it is probably a silver tankard of wine.)

Unnoticed, Leslie Williams took *Spirit of Cutty Sark* ahead of the northern group of boats. He logged his arrival opposite the Lizard at 0240, 5 minutes before Noel Bevan recorded it. At 0435 the Runnel Stone was 1 mile north of him; at 0700 the Seven Stones Lightvessel was a mile south, and at 1030 he took departure from Round Island, hard on the wind and heading west-south-west.

This lead was remarkable because just one week before the start, as he was nearing Plymouth on his qualifying cruise, Leslie had slipped on deck and lost the use of his right arm. An X-ray showed pieces of loose bone in the elbow and a doctor advised him that the only cure would be rest or an operation — what a difficult and lonely decision he must have made before removing the sling to come to the starting line with everyone else!

At 0915, shortly before he took departure, the wind was rising above force 5 in a short, rough sea. He had to tackle his first sail change — 860 square feet of genoa to be replaced by 500 square feet of jib. Behind him, however, several boats were already in trouble.

4 Trouble in plenty *2 - 5 June*

About 1600 on Sunday 2nd June Michael Richey was "awakened by a trumpeting to see poor Joan de Kat (in *Yaksha*) limping back under reefed main, with a broken forestay. I wondered if I should have circled him and offered help, but there was nothing much I could do. I wondered where he would end up: perhaps Britanny where he comes from". Joan de Kat put in to Braye Harbour, Alderney, rejoining the race when a mast band had been repaired.

In the early hours of that morning one repair had already been completed at sea — Bill Howell had replaced a servo blade. A number of boats were fitted with servo blades as part of their vaned steering; it was advisable to carry spares because the blades are vulnerable to floating debris from ahead and sudden forces of the sea from the side. Bill's blade had apparently been snapped off by a wave striking it sideways in a force 5 wind.

He noted in his log that "*Voortrekker* passed me while I was replacing the servo blade . . . going great guns under reefed main and big genoa, porpoising a lot and giving Dalling a rough ride!" *Voortrekker's* light displacement hull could throw a surfing wave 12 feet above her deck; resembling a rooster's tail, it would curve down to crash on the deck through the mizzen rigging. The surfing speed could rise to 14 knots — in bursts the speedometer would indicate 20. Bruce Dalling also had *Raph* in sight, and he slowly worked his way ahead of both boats.

The next morning Bruce had his own set back while he was reefing the mainsail; the halyard was in his left hand and the reefing handle in his right — without warning the bronze pin holding the gear train to the mast sheared. The roller-reefing

Photo: Dave Evans

The competitors gathered in Plymouth the day before leaving.
Back Row: (left to right) Bill Howell (Australia) *Golden Cockerel*, Bruce Dalling (S. Africa) *Voortrekker*, Bernard Rodriquez (U.S.A.) *Amistad*, Tom Follett (U.S.A.) *Cheers*, David Pyle (U.K.) *Atlantis III*, Michael Richey (U.K.) *Jester*, Geoffrey Williams (U.K.) *Sir Thomas Lipton*, William Wallin (Sweden) *Wileca*, Edith Baumann (W. Germany) *Koala III*, Michael Pulsford (U.K.) *White Ghost*, Leslie Williams (U.K.) *Spirit of Cutty Sark*, Eric Willis (U.K.) *Coila*, Egon Hiennemann (W. Germany) *Aye-Aye*, Claus Hehner (W. Germany) *Mex*, Eric Tabarly (France) *Pen Duick IV*, Lionel Paillard (France) *La Delirante*, Bernard Waquet (France) *Tamouré*, Sandy Munro (U.K.) *Ocean Highlander*, André Foëzon (France) *Sylvia II*.
Middle Row: (left to right) Joan de Kat (France) *Yaksha*, Nigel Burgess (U.K.) *Dogwatch*, Stephen Pakenham (U.K.) *Rob Roy*, Noel Bevan (U.K.) *Myth of Malham*, Martin Minter-Kemp (U.K.) *Gancia Girl*, Bertrand de Castelbajac (France) *Maxine*, Alex Carozzo (Italy) *San Giorgio*, Bertil Enbom (Sweden) *Fione*, Colin Forbes (U.K.) *Startled Faun*, Robert Wingate (U.K.) *Zeevalk*, Brian Cooke (U.K.) *Opus*, Alain Gliksman (France) *Raph*, Marc Cuiklinski (France) *Ambrima*.
In front (left to right) Jean Yves Terlain (France) *Maguelonne*, Åke Mattsson (Sweden) *Goodwin II*, Guy Piazzini (Switzerland) *Gunthur III*.

The fleet approaches Plymouth Breakwater. *Photo: Chris Smith.*

Sir Thomas Lipton (44), *Rob Roy* (7), *La Delirante* (40) and *Voortrekker* (2).
Photo: Eileen Ramsey.

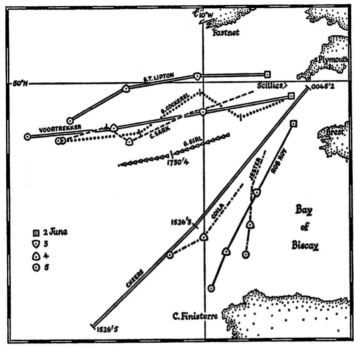

2–5 June

mechanism fell away in pieces, leaving the boom free to drop onto the deck and over the side, smashing a ventilator on the way. The mainsail was dragged down out of its track, into the sea with the boom where it trailed out, held by the mainsheet; the halyard was wrenched from Bruce's left hand, and it shot up the mast.

After 3 hours it was sorted out. The halyard had luckily jammed in the deck light half way up the mast — it is much easier to climb a mast as far as the cross-trees rather than go to the top. Bruce secured a lashing round the boom and, from it, a handy billy to the heel of the mast — this purchased the boom hard to the mast.

Pen Duick IV had arrived back in Plymouth earlier that morning, substantially damaged. After missing a ship by less than 30 yards, Eric Tabarly had gone below to brew some coffee — 15 minutes later he did hit another ship, at speed.

Aircraft artificers came to help him, from the Royal Naval

B

Engineering College, Manadon; they worked with magnificent speed to make good a 10-foot rip in his starboard hull (made of aluminium), while men from Mashford's Shipyard repaired the mizzen rigging. When the work was nearly completed, the mainmast rigging was seen to be faulty.

While the two teams were working on *Pen Duick IV*, Tom Follett was sailing *Cheers* the greatest distance from Plymouth. He had taken a south-west course across the face of the Bay of Biscay, and was now virtually committed to some form of southerly route. In his part of the ocean, Monday 3rd June was a warm, hazy day with a gentle breeze from the north-west. A second sunsight at 1526 placed him 160 miles north-north-west of Cape Finisterre.

Cheers was sailing on course without the assistance of vaned steering, an art which Martin Minter-Kemp was learning the hard way — he could not control his course in a gusty wind.

Eric Willis in the trimaran *Coila* had already come to terms with this problem. For the first 18 hours of the race his vaned steering had worked well, but when the heavy weather came in with big seas, *Coila* was accelerating from 8 to 18 knots down the waves — this brought the apparent wind round so fast that *Coila* was pulling her helm hard up and hitting the troughs broadside on.

"This not being terribly funny, I automatically worked the quick release gear and both lots of self-steering, one from each side, were jettisoned. I went on with two pieces of shock cord on the steering, and this was so satisfactory that she would go for as much as 18 hours without touching the helm — certainly not wandering much more than 5°. I had already done more than 600 miles in extremely heavy weather before the self-steering was fitted, on the principle that I would be quite happy to work on the shock cord if the self-steering gear was not up to standard."

Martin Minter-Kemp spent some four days without sleep trying to make his vane gear work. Finally he disconnected it, lashed the helm and went below to cook a meal and then sleep, leaving *Gancia Girl* to look after herself before turning back to England — "I was thoroughly depressed."

"I realised after about 20 minutes that she was sailing herself, and in fact the vane gear need not have been used at all. I completed the race on a lashed helm with adjustments to the mizzen and jibs. Without a ketch rig that would have been completely impossible. The mizzen is a wonderful sail for steadying, and by trimming the sheets down to half an inch at a time it was possible to sail her within 5° of the desired course."

In a monohull sloop one cannot expect such directional stability, and Egon Hienemann sailed *Aye-Aye* into Falmouth for advice on his particular vaned steering problems. When he telephoned Germany he learned that the designer of his vane gear was on holiday; then his beautiful young wife came on board, to whom he had been married but a month — Egon Hienemann retired from the race.

A competitor unsettled even before the start was the Frenchman, Commandant Waquet. He was muttering darkly when an Air France strike was threatened; then the strike materialised, and he let it be known that his trimaran, *Tamouré*, was too small to carry the navigational equipment needed to be independent — he had expected the aircrews of Air France to provide his chart positions (I am told that he would have transmitted at intervals to a passing aircraft to provide it with a series of bearings of his voice, the intersection of these bearings being his position.)

Despite this setback he started properly with everyone else, but it was subsequently learned that he sailed straight home to Brest.

Robert Wingate sailed *Zeevalk* into Plymouth on Tuesday 4th June with water slopping around his stores. He sailed three times for the race, and finally retired in Penzance on the 19th.

Three attempts were also made by Michael Pulsford, Leading Aircraftsman in the Royal Air Force. He had built his boat himself, the schooner trimaran *White Ghost*. He retired in Plymouth on Thursday 4th July.

William Wallin retired after five days, writing a charmingly frank explanation to the Royal Western Yacht Club: he had found the north Atlantic too cold. As he was Swedish, one might be suprised; but apparently he had spent all his sea career in the Far East, in hot climates. (William Wallin was reported lost at sea in 1969; his boat, *Vagabond*, was found empty near the Azores — he was crossing the Atlantic singlehanded, bound for Australia.)

Leslie Williams was discovering the limitations imposed by the injury to his right elbow. Before he took departure from the Scillies he was forced into battle with his large genoa; it took 45 minutes to change down to a smaller headsail while the wind was rising above force 5 in a difficult sea — his injured arm "took an awful hammering". The rest of that day the wind remained strong, and the 15 tons of *Spirit of Cutty Sark* forced their way westward, maintaining a lead on the direct route.

Early the next day–Monday 3rd June–the wind began to drop. By 0400 it was down to force 3, and 1½ hours later Leslie had reset his large genoa. The wind began to increase again; this time Leslie set himself the one-armed task of gathering the flogging billows of his large genoa while the wind was still force 4. The smaller sail was then set for nearly 3 hours before the wind filled in to force 5. He was under-canvassed. Bruce Dalling overhauled him during that day or the following night, despite his own trouble with broken reefing gear.

The next day the wind followed much the same pattern: it began dwindling in the early hours and at 0600 Leslie was becalmed for about an hour. At 0930 he hoisted the large genoa — the wind promptly blew up! This time he held on with the big sail. By 1400 it was blowing force 6, and at 1430 he began the headsail change. He broke off in the middle to reef the mainsail; he used his right arm to steady himself against the sail while his left arm rolled the boom six times round.

At 1530 the smaller genoa was set. The exertion had been too great for his injured elbow, and he stowed the large genoa in the cabin, feeling that it could be used no more. By 1900 the wind had dropped to force 4 — he was paying a heavy price for one quick slip on the deck.

At 0410 that morning Tom Follett had slipped on board *Cheers* while setting a jib. He fell against a winch, and later wrote in his log, "feels like a broken rib or two."

I do not know how many of us were seasick in the first few days, but I guess a good number! As the wind rose during the first night of the race I descended heavily to my bunk and there succumbed yet again. (I have never been seasick in a big ship, but often in a yacht!)

Resistance to seasickness can be greatly reduced by a nervous mind or tired body. If we were unaware of anxiety, our exhaustion was obvious — many of us put to sea to recover from the effort of the preparations.

I had been short on sleep for many weeks. Now I was prostrate for most of two days, unable to hold down food or drink; but a merciful succession of incidents kept rousing me from my miserable lethargy.

Rob Roy was moving too fast for her log: I trailed a longer line to stop the spinner jumping from the water. The steering lines–part of the vane gear–chafed through twice: I shackled two swivel blocks on the tiller and reled new lines through them. The leeward line then survived; the weather line continued to look painful, but the interval was longer before a strand broke round the block. The radar reflector pulled out its halyard — it crashed onto the deck 20 feet below and went overboard to trail on its cleated downhaul; the noise below as it hit the deck was a salutary shock!

After each incident I read the compass and log to plot a dead reckoning on the chart, but I was straying well to the south of my intended track. When at last I forced my fuddled mind to listen to Consol bearings, I entered the time as "17115" on Monday 3th June; I crossed the bearings some 125 miles north-west of my real position, and as the wind faded in a local anti-cyclone I edged my course further south towards Cape Finisterre.

Michael Richey, in clear mind, was alive to the difficult position of *Jester*. At 0240 on Tuesday 4th June he wrote, "A black night in which I am embayed — rain, gloom, apprehension on board. I do not seem to lay a course on either tack which will get me out of the Bay of Biscay — a classic situation, but I do not see what I could have done to prevent it. I suppose I should have gone hard on the wind earlier, but it grates a bit with several thousand miles to go" — *Jester's* lugsail is not particularly close-winded in fresh winds such as were blowing.

Our two problems were slight compared with the unfortunate Sandy Munro — his mast collapsed before his eyes. At the time it happened he was standing in his spacious cockpit, telling his tape recorder about the misbehaviour of his vane gear ("the bloody blade keeps jumping out"). His voice continued quietly, "Oh dear! the mast has gone — further report following."

He had sailed *Ocean Highlander* hard during the winter before the race to prove her in tough conditions. In the spring he secured a contract with a newspaper, and telephoned a chandlery to order insulators for converting a backstay into a transmitting aerial. He is certain in his own mind that he specified a breaking strain of 5 tons; the insulators supplied apparently had a breaking strain of 5,000 lbs (2.2 tons.) I am told that this telephone conversation nearly became the subject of an interesting court case because the first strong push of wind abaft the beam snapped the insulators, and the mast collapsed forwards from a break at the lower shrouds. *Gancia Girl* had been fitted with similar insulators, but they were spotted at Mashford's Shipyard and replaced. Sandy Munro sailed home under a jury rig.

At dawn on Wednesday 5th June Tom Follett was nearing the latitude of Cape Finisterre; by tradition one crosses this line southwards into warmer weather. His chest now felt loose, not broken. A gentle breeze was blowing, and at 0700 he went over the side to bathe in the sea. The sun, shining from a cloudless sky, soon dried him and he dressed in clean clothes.

North on the direct route, Bill Howell had been writing, "An awful night! A bumpy ride that gave me nightmares as I dozed off in cat-naps. I dreamed of hurricanes. I dreamed of shipwreck and capsize" — the difference between the two routes is becoming clear!

Later that day, we heard on a BBC newsflash that Eric Tabarly was finally out of the race. After leaving Plymouth, Eric had met increased problems with the vibrating of his steering gear when *Pen Duick IV* was moving at speed. He turned into Newlyn to attempt a quick repair; when he had to turn back the third time he decided to retire.

I believe that Eric Tabarly would have won the race with ease had he sailed without mishap in *Pen Duick IV*. As it was, there was now the probability of a close contest.

Bruce Dalling was leading on the direct route by about 50 miles. He did not know the north Atlantic well as Bill

Howell did, and this was his reaction to it — "My goodness, but this is a bleak and forbidding ocean — fine drizzle, fog, cold and a predominant grey colour which never ever seems to turn blue. And it is a restless confused ocean too, with little regularity in its motion — not a place I will come back to readily. I can understand now why Hasler says it tones up his nervous system . . . the wind has been forward of the beam the whole race so far — have only had the sheets started for a period of 6 hours . . . my introduction to the north Atlantic has not exactly been a frivolous one . . . I miss warmth and the sun."

Bruce has an athletic determination tempered by a capable intellect. Born in the Transvaal 29 years before the race, he has spent most of his life in Natal where he read for a degree in agriculture at Pietermaritzburg University. During a spell in London he signed on to become a police inspector in Hong Kong, and while there for a $3\frac{1}{2}$ year commission he was in command of a penetration patrol unit; he also had the Vertue, *Carina*, built by Cheoy Lee, and in February 1966 sailed her singlehanded the 8,000-mile passage to Durban.

After the race he was returning to Pietermaritzburg to complete a further degree in philosophy and theology: the experience of being alone from Hong Kong to Durban had raised fundamental questions in his mind which he hoped would be answered by a study of theology.

Calculating through a traverse table with the given chart positions, at 1200 on the 5th Bruce Dalling was 556 miles from the starting line; at 1527 Tom Follett was 638 miles from it (Bruce had logged a distance of 670 miles, the extra mileage being caused by the head winds he was meeting.)

Bruce and Tom were matched against each other, and behind them on both routes the boats were forming patterns which would give a succession of contests across the Atlantic Ocean.

5 The long leg south   *5 - 9 June*

Leslie Williams and Bill Howell recorded noon positions on the 5th which were close together; at dawn on the 6th they were becalmed and then at 0600 both noted down that a breeze was filling in. At the same time Bill wrote, "A sail–a big yacht by the look of it–on western horizon a couple of miles ahead of me. Soon swallowed by the mist."

Bill scarcely seemed to be excited, but his writing continued, "Not feeling too grand this morning. Have the squirts."

The early morning can be the time of lowest ebb; one has sailed on through the dark, trying both to maintain daylight performance and also sleep as the conditions allow. Lying down when the boat is bouncing about, one's stomach can feel like a balloon filled with soft jelly, and with an inch of clearance all round (stand up, and the jelly settles down comfortably at once.) By force of habit one has eaten normally during the day and then snacks through the night do little to steady an ailing stomach.

Leslie also noted the sighting at 0600 — "Sail astern. Large ketch without mizzen." At 0730 Bill saw Leslie again, and after a further 3 miles he wrote that he was "catching up on the other yacht very fast, and passing to windward of him. Doing comfortably 7 knots to windward, apparent wind 9–10 knots." During that hour Leslie logged 3 miles against Bill's 7; in these conditions he was thoroughly caught without his big genoa set — at the end of the previous day he had ruefully written in his logbook, "Today's mistake: should have set second genoa all day (arm too weak)." A further 10 miles, and Bill wrote, "We are passing the monohull, going to windward of him. Feeling queasy."

The stronger wind which Leslie needed then arrived by

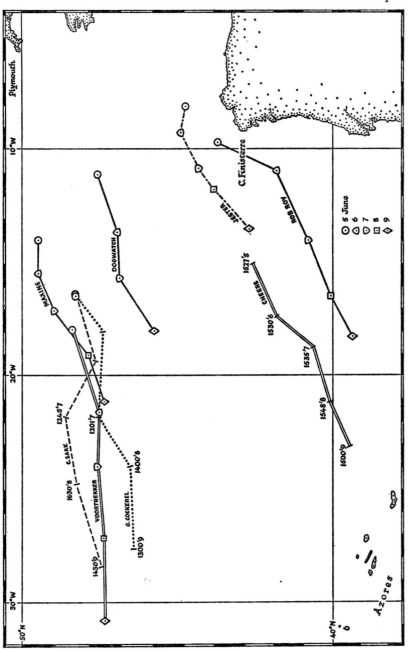

5–9 June

midday, and he sailed into it at 8 knots. During the afternoon a front passed over them, bringing rain. After dark Bill "had to clamber into a wet suit to tie down the genoa staysail with yet another sail tie as a bunt of the sail had broken loose and was flapping up from the foredeck like a demented ghost."

It is interesting to compare their comments in these rougher conditions. The next morning Bill wrote, "Last night was awful for me, but the big monohulls must have skied through it and stolen a march on me.

"0930 — have changed to No. 4 genoa, and main with two rolls. Taking a hell of a pounding as we thrash to windward at 6½ knots. My heart is awhirl! This big cat is a handful and needs to be watched all the time. This non-stop Round the World is just *not* on in this boat. I am going to be a nervous and physical wreck by the time I reach Newport. I would be dead before I was half-way round the world.

"1015 — have just had breakfast — spaghetti thrown in with last night's stew, and coffee. Cannot do anything else except throw cans into the pot in this weather — bash! bash! bash! bash into headwinds. Difficult enough to eat food, let alone prepare it!"

Leslie simply wrote, "A really forcing 7 knots to windward well rolled in." During that day, the 7th, he assessed from reports the positions of the leaders as "Bruce Dalling 24°W? Others 22°W". The 'others'–four boats roughly in line behind *Voortrekker*–were *Raph*, *Sir Thomas Lipton*, *Spirit of Cutty Sark* and *Golden Cockerel*.

The South African blood flowing through Bruce's veins was finding the lead chilly — "It's really cold now — I'm wearing 2 pairs of socks, quilted underwear, ordinary underwear, towel shirt, jersey and oilskins. Trouble is they are all damp."

The previous day *Raph* and *Sir Thomas Lipton* had both been sighted by aircraft, and *Raph* appeared to be slightly ahead. In the stronger head winds following their meeting, *Spirit of Cutty Sark* was moving ahead once more from *Golden Cockerel*.

Leslie greeted the start of the 8th as "a bleak grey morning — fog, drizzle, visibility ½ mile, ugh!" At dusk that day, however, *Spirit of Cutty Sark* had a light diversion: as Leslie was taking off his oilskins in the doghouse, he was startled when the window suddenly filled with a greeny black mass; as he leapt into the cockpit, expecting a collision, the boat was jolted sideways. At first there was nothing to be seen; then he saw a huge whale fluke sink beneath the waves.

It was a Saturday, and Bill Howell had been listening to the commentary on the first Test Match between Australia and England. He enjoyed listening to the BBC — "It gives me a line to London which I love, and which is definitely my home." That day completed the first week of the race, and Bill had covered 800 miles. 400 miles to the south of him, Tom Follett had covered 1,000 miles along the Azores route, and yet his position was east of Bill's.

The boats sailing the Azores route were in the middle of their long leg to the south. To many people this first leg makes a mockery of the route, as though a man had agreed to compete in a one-mile race round an athletic track, running the first lap in the outside lane.

Those who sail the Azores route are gambling on prevailing weather conditions in which boats on the direct route labour into awkward seas thrown up by head winds, with the added backward set of the Atlantic Current. This means that the one-mile runner has deliberately chosen the outside lane because he expects that the runners on the inside of the track will be forced to zigzag through soft and pitted cinder.

This race had opened out from Plymouth in prevailing conditions and the boats on the Azores route had done little or no tacking through relatively gentle seas. At the end of the first week *Rob Roy* had logged 860 miles, some 60 miles more than the larger *Golden Cockerel*, but *Rob Roy* was not buffeting against difficult head seas.

Three boats well matched were *Maxine*, *Dogwatch* and *Rob Roy*. The longest of the three at 34.7 feet was the monohull sloop *Maxine*, sailing on the direct route. She is a Saxon-class boat–designed by Alan Buchanan–built at Burnham-on-Crouch in 1961 by R. J. Prior and Sons. She might be described as 'good solid English racing type.' There is also something distinctly 'good and solid' about Count Bertrand de Castelbajac who sailed her — his family title has its origin in the time of the First Crusade to Jerusalem; his eyes look steadily with a relaxed authority that speaks of the generations of leadership. The family Chateau de Castelbajac stands 1,500 feet above the

Bay of Biscay on the foothills of the Pyrenees. As Bertrand is not the eldest son, he has his own estate in the Bordeaux district; it is in the area of St Emilion and Pomerol and there at the Chateau Moulinet five families tend a 30-acre vineyard for him ("my first passion, more than the sea perhaps".) He had a bottle of his claret for each day at sea and a friend had provided white wine, likewise a bottle for each day.

During the morning of the 6th–at the same time as Bill Howell and Leslie Williams were in sight of each other–Bertrand was watching Jean Yves Terlain ahead in *Maguelonne*, while Jean Yves looked backwards at him and forwards to the blue sails of *Opus*.

Rob Roy is 32 feet long. She was one of the last boats built by George Feltham and his two sons at Portsmouth, in 1956. She has an interesting pedigree: Spen King, son of the first owner of the pre-war Robert Clark–designed *Ortac*, decided to design a smaller boat for himself on similar lines. He took his lines to George Feltham, who then in effect became co-designer with him and Robert Clark.

Rob Roy was the third of the class to be built; Colonel Tweed, retired from the Royal Marines, designed the ketch rig — a fourth designer! The class was respected in racing circles for being stable and remarkably dry in a seaway. It is time to shorten sail in *Rob Roy* when she heels to 25°; I have never been wet to the skin while aboard her, nor has the cabin become damp.

There was an advantage for the ketch rig in this race: the Race Committee handicapped the monohulls on their L measurement only, i.e., the measurement of the hull, disregarding the sail plan (this was to allow freedom for the development of new ideas.) *Rob Roy* was carrying three sizes of main spinnaker, a mizzen spinnaker and three sizes of mizzen staysail. Free winds on the Azores route can help the ketch to realize its potential. Comparing the tracks of *Maxine* and *Rob Roy* at this period, one can imagine both boats to be on the arm of a giant windmill revolving round the north pole — *Rob Roy* was swinging round faster, further out on the arm.

Dogwatch was between *Maxine* and *Rob Roy*, following the northern edge of the Azores route. The weather was not being kind to Nigel Burgess — at 0100 on the 7th it was "blowing like hell," but on the 8th he was becalmed from 0700 to 1800; stationary under menacing clouds, he recorded no midday position, but instead busied himself in his 'Saturday Make & Mend': "really quite successful, for I managed to wash my hair, and shave."

If *Dogwatch* was to take 38 days 12 hours to reach Newport, then to equal her on handicap *Rob Roy* would have to arrive 17.7 hours ahead, and *Maxine* 25.6 hours. The sagging position of *Dogwatch* at this stage had temporarily used up the time she had to spare, but it reflected little more than her local calm on the 8th.

These local calms can affect positions in the race more than anything else except retirement itself. *Rob Roy* escaped trouble in the Bay of Biscay; it started early on the 4th, and by midday I was hoisting different light weather headsails attempting to keep the boat moving. A steady wind, however light, would fill the largest genoa, but when it began to flap it needed replacing with a smaller yankee ghoster less likely to chafe against the rigging. The two sails required frequent exchanging, and a similar exchange was made with two sizes of mizzen staysail.

By 0130 on 5th June I was becalmed — I dropped all sails to save them from chafe; I had hardly moved forwards since sunset. It seemed so pointless to have struggled during the past 18 hours to keep the boat moving when the effort ended like this. I watched a whale slowly circle to investiagte me — it came to within a few inches, first on the port side and then on the starboard, and then abruptly left.

At 0315 there was a stir from the west, and the yankee ghoster was up quickly to catch it. Almost at once it was replaced with the large ghosting genoa, and then I hoisted the mainsail, mizzen and mizzen staysail. It felt as though a heavy, stifling weight had suddenly been lifted as the bow wave chuckled back along the sides of the boat — we were moving at more than 3 knots. Perversely, I was still rebellious about working hard for those 18 hours — now I was asking why I had bothered when a firm wind was coming anyway!

I had no idea at the time that I had groped my way out of the edge of the calm, leaving the smaller *Jester* to wallow in it.

Jester's track for this period shows clearly her lean progress as she slowly rounded the north-west corner of Spain — her single lugsail was at a disadvantage in these conditions. *Rob Roy* sailed on southwards to enter the favourable south-flowing Portugal Current and pick up the prevailing north wind blowing down that coast.

Late in the afternoon of the 8th *Jester* also found the north wind. "I had by now assumed that 3–4 days of calm had killed my chances in the race, and this gave me a certain liberty to play about."

Michael Richey began an intellectual exercise appropriate to his specialist ability. He has been Executive Secretary to the Institute of Navigation since its inception in 1946, and is also widely regarded as the world's leading navigator in offshore racing.

"I could now take either the route north of the Azores, or the way below latitude 28°, but a final decision must be made before I fall between either stool by steering a compromise course. It worried me that Maury, who after all studied sailing ships' routes as no one had before, was completely silent about the southern route. On the other hand, he does say, I think, that his routes ignore current, which may well have been feasible for vessels capable of 12–14 knots. I computed the distances from my position off Cape Villano to Nantucket by Great Circle, rhumb line (or Maury's route) and the Trades. They were respectively 2,600, 2,800, and 4,000 miles. Interpolating from the British Pilot Chart values for current, head winds, calms, bad weather etc., the durations of passage each seemed to be about the same: 40 days. Necessarily some of the factors were derived completely arbitrarily and of course, for example, if you got following winds instead of head winds on the rhumb, it would be by far the best route. On the other hand I decided finally to try the southern on the grounds that *Jester* would sail at her fastest with following winds and, other things being equal, this should clip a day or two off the notional passage time. I confess also to an intellectual curiosity about this route."

Jester was about to be the first yacht in three races to sail far enough south to cross by the famous north-east Trade Wind; it had always been regarded as giving a possible route,

but no one had previously found the courage or inclination to
actually try it.

As *Jester* began to enjoy the drive of the Portuguese Trade
Wind, *Rob Roy* was leaving it for the Azores. The Pilot chart
clearly warns that the approach to the Azores from the east is
through an area with a relatively high proportion of calms and
light airs. I began to feel the effect of this on the 7th, and
it felt much too soon! The wind backed from north to north-
north-west, and started fading away; at 0630 I set the largest
mizzen staysail and, at 0730 for the first time, the largest main
spinnaker.

I kept moving well enough through that day and night, but
the mounting sun of the following day seemed to kill the wind.
By 1300 *Rob Roy* was struggling in light airs which lasted until
after midnight. During the afternoon I was barely moving.
I dropped the mainsail, and boomed out the spinnaker on
both sides, attempting to keep it filled and steady. In light
following conditions, when a boat is rolling to a gentle swell,
it can seem best to concentrate on the spinnaker; the material
of the mainsail is too heavy to be shaped by the wind — it
slats to and fro spoiling the flow of air to the spinnaker. I
dropped the mizzen staysail as well. The spinnaker continued
to curtsey from side to side in time with the roll, but it ballooned
out sufficiently to keep our steerage way.

On a day like this the wind is rarely steady. A slight increase,
and hope would hoist the mainsail and mizzen staysail — but
not for long! The mizzen could be quietly left up in all this
juggling — not large enough to slat violently, its boom could
be held by a foreguy winched against the backward pull of
sheets.

It was thirsty work, but not for alcohol because I feel winded
if exertion follows a drink — I find spirits worse for this than
beer. The tins of fruit juice were stowed low in *Rob Roy's*
bilges; the sea flowing past them the other side of the planking
kept them cool, and a pineapple juice was welcome during
a pause in the sail changing.

The next trick of the wind was to back further. The leeward
pole on the spinnaker was unshipped and stowed in its chocks,
and the windward pole eased forward until it nearly met the
forestay; polythene sheeting was secured round the shrouds to

prevent the soft line of the sheet from chafing itself. The backing wind continued round until, from the beam, it began to collapse the spinnaker sideways — down it came to be replaced by the large ghosting genoa, and all the sails behind the genoa went up to work on the draught it was deflecting back along the boat. With the rolling reduced by the beam wind, *Rob Roy* sailed at a wavering $3\frac{1}{2}$ knots.

Why struggle so to woo the fickle wind? The answer is simple. The 24-hour run through this day was 93 miles; if I had only sailed to the obvious patches of wind the run might have been 40 miles less. The 24-hour run for *Rob Roy* in a spanking breeze might be 130 miles if one set a cruising weight of canvas; the effort to race to the good wind might then increase the run by 10 miles. This suggests that the extra effort during one day of light winds can gain as much as the extra effort over four days of fresh winds.

The same thoughts must have come to Nigel Burgess caught in light airs — he wrote, "I must push *Dogwatch* harder, for this is a race and not a cruise. (It is also a holiday!)"

About 200 miles ahead of *Rob Roy*, *Cheers* reached the area of light winds a good day sooner. At 0815 on the 6th Tom Follett seemed to be anticipating it — "Nice and warm. Very pleasant, but not fast sailing." At 0930 it had arrived — "Flat calm. Sun bathing on deck." Aboard *Cheers* the reaction to this situation was evidently not the same as aboard *Rob Roy*, but *Cheers* carried five sails only compared to *Rob Roy*'s 16: apart from his mainsail and mizzen, Tom had just three jibs to set flying; but note that his 40-foot proa weighed a little over a ton compared to *Rob Roy*'s 32 feet on 7 tons.

Weight was Tom's trump suit, and the next day he began nonchalantly to play the cards: "0700 — threw overboard some excess baggage." This was merely some tins of unopened food — a low card. The ace came at 1300 — "Dumped 5 gallons of fresh water." This was half the original 10 gallons with which he had left Plymouth. He had used but 2 gallons crossing from the West Indies to England in April. "I only took 10 gallons on the race because I thought they might go up in smoke if I told them I was only taking 5."

At the start of the race there were probably very few people in England who understood one essential side of Tom's character

The crew of the French naval training vessel *Etoile* cheering Eric Tabarly in *Pen Duick IV.*   Photo : *Eileen Ramsay.*

Bruce Dalling–"all eyes at home are on me and it's a fearful responsibility."
Photo: Bob Salmon.

— he never wastes his energy, and if he were a camel he would survive on a very small hump! He fines away his food, equipment and navigation into models of economy. This, too, is his stamp as a very able seaman, relaxed and astute. Other men struggle valiantly in a gale while Tom sails quietly and fast in a safer, warmer part of the ocean.

For breakfast he would have just a tin of fruit juice or cup of chocolate, and for lunch one slice of bread, folded over something like cheese or salami (he dipped into a favourite bottle of pickled onions like Pooh into honey.) In the evening he would have his one conventional hot meal, from tins of meat and vegetables, while overnight he would munch dried fruit and nuts.

This menu followed his natural inclination; it was not the agonised self-discipline of the ascetic — he opened one tin of beer for lunch and another in the evening. He washed himself by bathing over the side, and only used his fresh water for making cocoa and the oatmeal which he ate about twice a week.

By midday on the 9th *Cheers*, intermittently becalmed, may look on the analysis chart to be hopelessly placed against *Voortrekker* — this is the risk of the long leg south to the Azores. If the direct route provides free winds while the Azores route meets trouble, this leg can be a complete disaster. In the 1964 race the approach to the Azores was through a gale while the direct route had favourable weather — the south-going boats had barely reached the Azores when Eric Tabarly arrived at Newport in *Pen Duick II*.

The position of *Cheers* in this race was, however, far from hopeless. The leading direct route boats had completed the first third of their race, and by averages the middle third was likely to throw up the worst weather. The middle third of the Azores route is by contrast likely to be its best stretch — positions can change dramatically.

6 A storm "from nowhere"
9 - 15 June

The Atlantic weather chart for midday 9th June shows a depression, designated Low N, passing well to the north of the boats on the direct route. A front from the centre of this Low was curving gracefully to the east and then southwards across several thousand miles of ocean.

If one tries to describe the origin of a particular depression, one soon realises that one is studying a chain of cause and effect going ever backwards. A depression moving eastwards across the north Atlantic tends to trail a front behind it, along which another depression develops. The secondary depression may repeat the process and so it continues.

Thus, on the weather chart for the 4th, Low M had been trailing a front which began to develop another Low. The new Low was a weakling at birth, and the 5th June chart does not show it. On the 6th, however, it reappeared as strongly depressed as its parent of 1,000 millibars, and on the 8th it had grown stronger still at 988 millibars. This was of course Low N, and it apparently developed three fronts, a warm one followed by two cold ones.

Low N did not provide attractive sailing weather on the 9th. Leslie Williams wrote, "Another bleak day. Low scud everywhere. Tantalising glimpse of watery sun every 2 hours or so . . . tempted to shake out rolls, but weather looks threatening every time I think about it. It is so easy to stay at a smooth 7 knots, with a falling barometer."

Later Leslie wrote, "Work work work — no sailing" but added, "Calmer this late afternoon — sun for 2 hours", and he called his home as it was his son Gareth's birthday. At 1630, shortly after the call, he changed down to storm jib with 10 rolls in the mainsail — "have a feeling about the

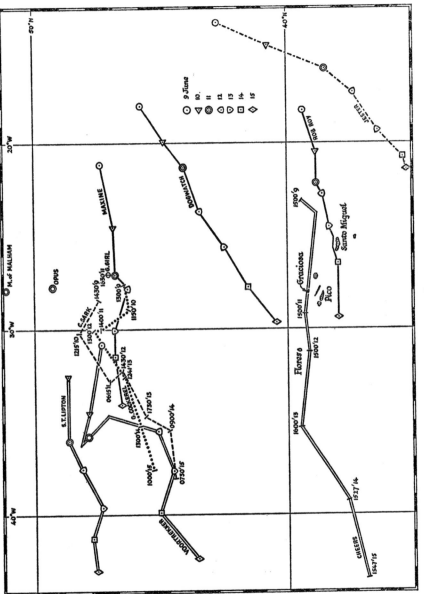

9–15 June

weather." An hour later he recorded, "A few vicious squalls now." The front apparently cleared him after about 2 hours, he shook out 6 of the rolls in the mainsail and set the working jib.

The front reached Bill Howell at dusk, the wind gusting to force 8. "I set about the difficult job of tying down a deep reef in the mizzen. It must have taken me a full $\frac{1}{2}$ hour and was quite the most dangerous job I have had to do this voyage as I had to hang over the end of the aft cross-bar to pull out the reefed clew." Bill summarized his feelings next morning — "Another bloody awful night, like always! The north Atlantic has really decided to get at me this time."

It seems that this front was becoming more vicious as it travelled eastwards. It struck Brian Cooke and Noel Bevan at about midnight. *Myth of Malham* came up into the wind and Noel found that the bottom casing of his self-steering gear had broken. He lowered his staysail and backed his jib to heave to. At 0300 the seams in his mainsail started parting in heavy rain. He remained hove to for 14 hours while he repaired the self-steering gear and stitched the mainsail. Brian Cooke was hove to from 0200 to 0700 on the 10th (without gear failure.) He had written at midnight, "It is now blowing force 8 without any doubt at all."

The direct route and Azores route boats do not normally share the same weather, but this front from Low N was an exception. At 0130 on the 10th Tom Follett lowered his mizzen in rain; the wind had been increasing for some hours. At 0415 he hoisted the mizzen again as the wind was dropping, but at 0530 the mizzen came down quickly when the wind veered from west-south-west to west-north-west and increased to force 7 on the passage of the front. 2 hours later the sun was shining, the barometer rising; the wind had dropped to force 6.

For *Rob Roy* the experience of the front was markedly different. By now it was weakening in the higher pressure to the south, but was also apparently twisting to lie in a more east-west direction. This would mean that *Rob Roy* passed along the front rather than across it. I was kept too busy to write much, but summarized by saying, "Day and night of fair winds and angry squalls with much sail changing."

During the 10th Bruce Dalling, leading the race, was

meeting the next gale force wind produced by Low N; he dropped his mainsail at 0800, sailing into it under yankee and mizzen. It reached Leslie Williams at 0900, easing at about 1700 to force 6–7. Again, this front was intensifying at first as it travelled eastwards. Bill Howell was struck by a line squall which shot the wind up to force 10 — "I clung on, all sheets eased, and rode out the blow." At midday he wrote, "This morning has been a succession of blinding line squalls and torrential rain. Wind just spurts up from 25 knots to 40 knots and over, and really it's quite dangerous. I rode through a terrifying sequence of these about one every ½ hour, and then I decided that it was just too dangerous for a singlehander in a multihull under the conditions. So I put up the storm jib and reefed mizzen, and we are just jogging along to the north at about 1½ knots. However, when these line squalls strike, the speed goes up to 5 knots. I have decided that the only seaman-like thing to do is to sit tight and to wait for these conditions to moderate . . . those damned monohulls must be getting away from me in these conditions."

At 1830 Bill wrote, "Wind is still strong force 6. Yacht lying nicely though only averaging about 2 knots . . . to force the ship to windward against these house walls of solid water would have to invite hull damage . . . it is so peaceful and pleasant in the cabin with the doors locked and the hatch pulled to, that I keep on poking my head out, thinking that the conditions have moderated. But they haven't — so I pull my head in again and resign myself to this slow, but safe and pleasant progress." At 2030 he lowered the storm jib and mizzen, and hoisted a reefed mainsail and working jib which brought the speed up to 7½ knots.

As every Englishman knows, the weather delights in in-consistency. At 1500, when one would have expected Brian Cooke to be in the thick of it, he wrote, "I have the charcoal stove going for the first time, not because it is cold, but in an attempt to dry things out a bit. It is unbelievable that 6 hours ago all hell was let loose on me; now it's a lovely sunny after-noon with a force 3–4 south-west breeze." At 1230 Noel Bevan was also in sunshine, but with a westerly force 6 wind which at 1600 was up to force 7.

As Low M begat Low N, so Low N begat Low P: the

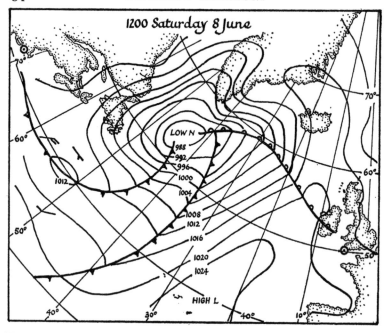

1200 Saturday 8 June

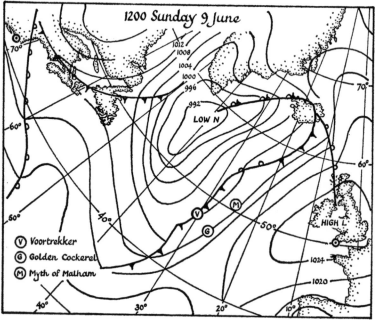

1200 Sunday 9 June

Ⓥ Voortrekker
Ⓖ Golden Cockerel
Ⓜ Myth of Malham

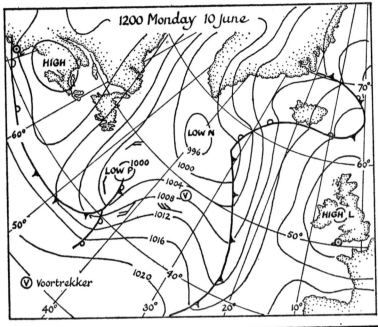

1200 Monday 10 June

HIGH

70°

60°

LOW N

996

LOW P 1000

1000

1004

1008 Ⓥ

1012

HIGH L

50°

60°

50°

1016

1020

40°

Ⓥ Voortrekker

40°   30°   20°   10°

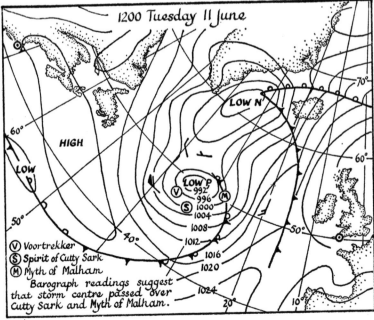

1200 Tuesday 11 June

70°

LOW N'

HIGH

60°

LOW

LOW P
992
996
Ⓥ
Ⓢ 1000
1004
Ⓜ

60°

50°

1008

40°

1012

50°

Ⓥ Voortrekker
Ⓢ Spirit of Cutty Sark
Ⓜ Myth of Malham
      Barograph readings suggest
that storm centre passed over
Cutty Sark and Myth of Malham.

1016

1020

1024

20°   10°

8th June weather chart shows a ball of thick cloud formed on the third front from Low N as it trails along the 38th parallel. The wind is circulating around the cloud, so another depression seems to be building up. The following day's chart does not show it, but on the 10th it reappears as Low P, ahead of the boats on the direct route.

Ashore, Low P was not thought to be of great significance on the 10th, but overnight a High on Nova Scotia was ridging rapidly 1,500 miles out into the Atlantic. Low P was also intensifying overnight — the ridge squeezed the already tightening isobars, greatly increasing the gradient wind.

For the singlehander, cut off from immediate help, it matters little what the wind is called when it blows really hard. Nowhere on the horizon offers the slightest respite or possible escape: everywhere the eye can see is a desolate expanse of rearing blue and tumbling white — like a mouse with a cat, you are alone with the gale. "Play with me," it seems to say — "there is nothing else you can do. Run wherever you like — you won't get away. I'm going to enjoy you–you cannot stop me–you are nothing against my strength and speed. Don't give up yet — here's my paw to help you. Be brave! The braver you are the longer we can play. That's better — bounce right up, then I knock you right down. It's unfair? I don't give a damn — play with me."

Is the sea cruel? Certainly it is for those who see its massive strength as fury, its heavy weather pounding as unfair violence.

Bruce Dalling was now sailing towards a howling wind and roaring sea which the seaman would call the "father and mother" of all storms. His story, devoid of complaint, is best taken up as a continuous experience from the day before.

"The gale (10th June) moderated at about dusk — and it left the boat soaking wet and in a shambles. Got the weather forecast and was not unduly worried by it as I thought the gale referred to was the one we had just been through. The sun came out, and, filled with that fantastic feeling of relief and reprieve that comes after a gale at sea, I cooked a meal of sausages, eggs, berries and had a couple of whiskies. Absolutely out I slumped into a sopping blanket and slept fitfully.

"The wind backed to south and then east and then north-east — I should have smelt a rat. In defence however I was so tired as to be almost jelly-like. But the thing that I did notice and did not pay enough heed to was the drop in the barometer after getting to 29.78. After being up a number of times during the night I awoke at 0500 with *Voortrekker* doing about 9 knots and well heeled over under yankee and mizzen only. One glance outside showed why — it was blowing a gale again. A glance at the barometer–my heart nearly stopped– 29.35! Within 30 minutes it was down to storm jib, and 30 minutes after that it was bare poles.

"The next 24 hours were the nightmare of a lifetime that will be the subject of my nightmares and will no doubt crop up in my thoughts even while awake. By 0800 the seas were as big as the ones in the Mozambique Channel that did me in while sailing *Carina*. I could no longer lie ahull as we were taking some bad ones. I came about and ran with the seas on the starboard quarter. I though of streaming a warp but decided against it as I wanted to have enough speed for positive steering but not enough to be dangerous. So we ran off south-east at about 5 knots. I stood below, steering with my legs and hanging onto the weather grip rail peering at the seas through the doghouse window. I judged the position of the boat by watching the streaks of foam on the water. This became difficult later as the continuous spray off the sea fogged the window up.

"I had to go forward to relash a spinnaker pole and one of the headsails, lashed on deck, which had broken adrift — and of course as soon as I left the helm she would not steer herself. She immediately came up into the wind beam on and took a couple of real bad ones over the top. I thought I was washed overboard — you could only hold your breath for that long under that kind of water. The waves were not all that steep, they were just enormous.

"In a period of about 30 seconds the main flogged a hole in itself. The height of the waves as a mean I conservatively estimated at 35 feet but there were some exceptional ones that must have been all of 50 feet. I prayed very hard during this storm and my prayers for survival were answered. There was a long period when the sea was far more white than any other colour — and if there was another colour it was black. The howl of the wind could only be beaten by the roar of the breaking waves. I did not dream that we could survive. And the thought that there were others perhaps going through the same agony only made it worse.

"We took some waves right over us–she would heel over to the horizontal and everything below would go a lovely deep blue colour–she seemed to broach under water and keep falling on her side. Then she would come up slowly shaking the water from her. It must have happened half a dozen times — nearly always because I wasn't concentrating on the helm. My mouth was permanently dry with fear and I nearly fainted a number of times from exhaustion.

"It started easing at about 1800 so I went on deck, tidied it all up, replaced the self-steering and set the yankee. I think that was the most courageous thing I have ever done in my life. It might not seem like it when reading this later, but I know what it took at the time.

"I estimate that I moved between 50 and 60 miles south-east (losing ground) as under bare poles she was averaging between 5 and 6 knots. I estimated the wind strength as a steady force 10 for a period of five hours, gusting force 11 or much higher. My Brookes and Gatehouse anemometer was hard against the 60 knot stop for some considerable period."

On the Beaufort Scale a wind of 64 knots or above is defined as a hurricane. As Bruce was running before the wind at 5–6 knots, it was clearly blowing at hurricane strength.

Once the yankee was set, he was able to head south-west, but his noon position on the 12th was back close to his noon longitude on the 10th. If the hurricane-force wind was sufficiently local, boats 200 miles behind him could have easily overtaken him during this 2 day period.

How did the other boats fare?

On Monday 10th June Leslie Williams was approximately 180 miles east of Bruce Dalling. He watched his barometer rising while the wind also rose, to gale force.

"I began to get worried that there was a heavy depression somewhere about and I decided to keep north in the hope of breaking through to the north-westerly stream, behind where I believed the centre to be. I set off on the northerly tack just after 0900 in gale force wind, very unpleasant, big seas. Barometer continued to rise, 1008 by evening and the wind fell to force 4 to 6 again. At about 2100 the winds suddenly shifted to the south-east and increased to gale force. I was quite happy with this, I thought I was now on top of the depression, I was making westerly, going very fast. If it was a bit dodgy I wasn't too worried. I had a good strong boat and a gale wasn't going to hurt her very much, and then suddenly the barometer began to drop very quickly down to 1002 by midnight — the wind had increased to about 50 knots. I looked at the mainsail and thought I wasn't going to be able to get it down, went below again and decided I'd have to get it down or the boat was going to do some damage to herself. I was going so fast through the water — well off the 10 knot speed, going more like a submarine than a boat on the surface. I was going so fast, with awful noise and lots of spray being driven horizontal, a rather frightening sight. I put the spreader lights on and everything looked grey, wild, and horrible. Eventually I hooked myself onto the life-line and went on deck.

"I eased out the boom just as much as I dared, took up a little on the topping lift and I got the main down, after a great fight. I was very, very happy to have it down and made the

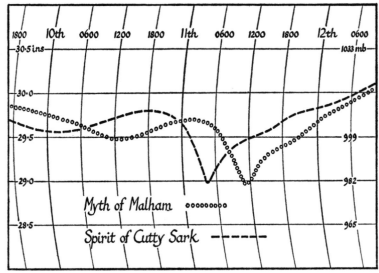

Myth of Malham barograph trace with *Spirit of Cutty Sark* barometer readings
superimposed.

best stow that I could, got the boom as low as it would go,
lashed it down securely and went back down below again,
thinking that all was over and settled now, and I could relax.
My arm was badly hurt, very weak and giving pain again
after this effort. I had still set the small high-footed number
3 jib and I thought that that would stand up to anything that
was likely to blow. I was rather wrong, the barometer continued
to drop — had gone down to 982 by 0400, a very considerable
drop. The wind had increased and was well off the scale on
the 60 knot anemometer, the needle wasn't even coming
back on the scale as the boat rolled away from the wind on the
big waves. I don't know what the wind force was, I think it
must have been 100 knots or so. The boat was going so fast
that she was completely in the water, everything was in the
water. On deck everything just looked white and flat —
horrible. I could see very little because of the spray, I wasn't
sure if it was spray or solid sheets of water, at times it felt more
like driven hail. The noise was tremendous and the speed
through the water tremendous, with awful jolts as we shot off
wave tops into chasms — just a horifying situation. I looked at
the jib and I thought it would be impossible to get it down

and then I looked again and saw how the boat was behaving. She was going right over on her beam, as she broached from time to time, the mast almost horizontal. I just had to try something. I didn't expect to live on the deck, I thought I would get washed away probably, but reasoned that I had to try because I would lose the boat anyway and wouldn't survive in the seas in a dinghy even if I could get it away.

"I tied myself on with my life-line to the wire running down the deck, a continuous life-wire from the cockpit to the bow. I remember feeling quite proud that I had remained calm and able to reason. I lay flat on the deck and tried to slow myself down as I was washed or blown forward. I grabbed the mast as I was floating by and my hand fortunately came onto the brake handle of the fore-halyard winch. Somewhere about this time, there came a sudden wind shift and the boat turned 180° almost instantaneously, just going around in a very tight circle. Looking back I saw the wind vane break off, as the stern came up through a wave, and a grinding noise coming from the gear, and then the boat started to jibe. As she jibed, the port side of the boat which I was on went under water. I was up to my neck in the water, hanging grimly onto the brake release handle — normally I can't get this off just by pulling with my hand alone, I have to put a handle onto it and I could not have got a handle in these conditions. The force of the water dragging me away was sufficient to release the brake handle and as the boat was jibing, the jib dropped a couple of feet on each jibe and very gradually came down. It was very horrifying, I would never have thought of jibing to get it down, I would have thought it was too dangerous and this strain on the rigging must have been tremendous. On one jibe I was up to my neck in water, on the other, in the air looking down the mast at the water. However, the sail came down after about eight jibes and I was able to lie on top of it and make a very temporary lashing to hold it onto the deck. The sail, all credit to Ratsey's, had stood up wonderfully to the strain, but the heavy Strenlite hanks holding it to the forestay were worn to a sliver. I got myself back into the cockpit, put the wheel hard over to windward, locked it there and left the boat lying ahull. I battened up the hatch and shut myself down below, very, very relieved. Although the storm had been frightening from the start, there had been some satisfaction earlier in that I was going at such a terrific speed in the right direction. Now with the wind shift, I'd obviously got the centre of the storm and I was lying ahull to the north-westerly wind and making a southerly course. The wind continued to back and turned to the west eventually, and I was making something like a south-easterly course, which of course, was just what I didn't want. I knew that to win the race I had to get over the top of this depression, or in fact, I knew I would have won the race if I could have got over the top. I was pretty desolate at this stage, everything just seemed to have slipped away from me. I lay ahull throughout the day, the wind gradually eased off to about 60 knots and continued to register between 50 and 60 knots for the rest of the day. The barometer rose quite quickly and was up to 1008 again by 2000. It was interesting to watch the anemometer as the boat was rolling. With the boat rolling into the wind the needle was going right off the clock again, as the boat rolled away from the wind lessening the relative wind at the mast-head, we were just reading down to 50 knots occasionally.

"Now the seas became nasty as the wind direction changed, so although the wind had eased off the waves were in fact getting worse and more dangerous and the crests were breaking awkwardly. I was taking some water, and my aft hatch wasn't quite strongly enough fastened, so I was doing quite a lot of pumping. I started the diesel so that I could charge my batteries and use an electric pump, but the engine ran for about 20 minutes and then packed in, which depressed me even further. During the afternoon, I was able to make radio contact and asked for a general warning to be broadcast for other boats behind — for this storm had not been forecast in the previous day's met information, and there were several boats which could well founder, if caught by this stuff unawares. I also put in a call home to have a word with the kids, just in case."

Bill Howell had his receiver switched on while Leslie Williams was talking — "He must be feeling homesick, ringing up his wife and speaking to his kid. Bad for morale!" About 100 miles behind Leslie, Bill was writing his own account of the storm. He was nearly through it — it had reached him shortly after

Leslie. 2245 — "Just had a succession of line squalls with increased wind but no rain — certainly not as bad as last night and yesterday. However, I am as nervous as a kitten and sat in the cockpit with the mainsheet in hand ready to fly it. The speed goes up to 10 knots."

2330 — "A discovery! We are going along quite well at 7-8 knots under working jib only. I dropped the reefed main and found that the speed dropped by 2 knots, but my goodness! what a difference for the yacht, even though she's still taking a pounding. Australia won the first Test Match by 159 runs.

"About 0100 I was awoken by the Hepplewhite gear releasing. It was pelting down a solid wall of rain, so I waited to clamber into my wet suit before going up to lower the main and jib.

"I was terrified by what I saw! The *Cockerel* was canted over sideways to the wind, which was 40-50 knots (force 10) on the indicator. The jib sheets had threaded out through the blocks on both sides (released by the Hepplewhite gear) and had bunched themselves into a big iron-hard ball of knotted Terylene flogging madly at the clew of the sail. The deck was being swept by giant combers — I could see their luminous white crests ranging up from out of the darkness.

"I decided to run her off, and with great trouble finally managed to haul her stern into the waves. I snapped in both vanes, and doused and bagged the jib after taking off the sheets which were knotted into a great ball as thick as my torso.

"All the time the wind was blowing harder and harder. She was still running comfortably at 8 knots before the blast as I pulled down the main — this didn't seem to make any difference as she ran before it under bare poles — still 8 knots. The wind indicator was over 40 knots, so the true wind must have been 50 knots or over.

"I could not run back on my path at this fantastic speed — I should lose days in the race. The mizzen was still reefed and furled, so I brought up the storm jib and managed to fight its hanks at the forestay. Blinding rain, and the noise was fantastic. Seas were 25-30 feet high, with their crests being torn off by the force of the wind. We were well above gale force 8–wind speed was more than 50 knots–it was whole gale 9 or storm force 10. I think it was the worst gale I have ever been in at sea. It was the most terrifying, as I was in fear of capsizing the big cat if I should make a wrong move. The self-steering gear made up my mind for me. It began steering erratically. I thought it was the steering lines and tried to adjust them through the cam cleats at the tiller leads, but it didn't make any difference.

"We slewed our stern to the seas as we ran down a big wave, and the sheer force of the wind overpowered both vanes and they jumped out from the worm gears, even though these were held down by shock cord.

"I tried steering by hand. It was a pitch black night, the air was full of spindrift or rain or both. She was heavy to steer with the steering blade in the water, and I was about to risk a quick dash aft to the tiller leads to let go the tiller lines when the blade jumped out of its patent release and cocked up out of the water, releasing the pressure. I don't think anything hit the blade–there isn't a mark on its leading edge–the pressure of the sea racing past just snapped it out. I don't see how this type of self-steering can work at these speeds, especially down wind, that these cats can do. The only answer seems to be to trail heavy warps astern to keep the speed down to one that the self-steering can manage. But perhaps then there is the danger of a bad poop . . . in any case, I was in a race, and I couldn't be racing away from the finishing line at 200 miles per day. Despite the unknown element of risk in rounding up in these conditions, I had to try to bring her head to wind. There was no question of selecting a so-called 'slick' — I couldn't see the waves, only the white spume of their crests as it flew at me in solid chunks.

"I brought her round, God knows how, just put down the tiller and tried to bring her up. She lay sideways on and refused to head higher. I remembered Juergen Wagner writing that *World Cat* hove to on the Cape Agulhas Banks under reefed mizzen and storm jib, and jogged gently forward, up and away in a rhythmic fashion, fronting the waves and then gliding sideways to them, but always going forwards.

"I decided to do the same.

"I raised the storm jib after a mighty battle to hank it on and reeve its sheets. The angle of heel increased alarmingly —

Yaksha–"rigging wire was stretched out in every plausible direction."

Photo: Eileen Ramsay.

Bill Howell   *Photo : Eileen Ramsay.*

I could not tell what it was, the clinometer was dancing
everywhere in the cockpit as the cat swayed up and down the
steep waves. It was obvious that her head was being pushed
away and that I had to raise the mizzen to push her nose up.

"Again, a battle to get that reefed mizzen up. The battens
kept catching under the stays — I would winch her up, then
have to drop the head, then winch again as the mizzen tended
to luff and flop, trying to catch the right moment when the
leech could clear the backstay. At last I managed to get it up.

"Now *Cockerel* was moving sideways to the seas at 4 knots.
I might be going in the right direction, but as she rose to the
top of each giant breaker, the storm hit the tiny storm sails
and heeled her over. Again I had visions of capsize and the
end of another singlehanded multihuller. I was glad that I
had shifted the water and heavy sails into the weather hull.

"There was only one thing to do, drop the jib and heave
to under mizzen alone, even though this might mean making
sternway and putting dangerous pressure on the rudders. It
was either that or lie-a-tri — and I remembered that Tom
Corkhill in his trimaran had been flipped over by the steep
face of a wave only a few months ago in the South Pacific, so I
didn't want to 'hull' it in these seas.

"I dropped the jib–should I say that I brought it down to
the deck as though it were a snapping, shrieking white tiger–
and subdued its snarls with gaskets to the safety net. Then I
tied down the tiller and let her heave to. And so she has been
since 0200, in fact possibly about 10 hours.

"She has lain quite happily, coming up to about 45° of the
wind and then bearing off to about 80°. She has been making
sternway, and drifting down wind at about 1 knot, but at
least she is giving to the wind and waves and not trying to
fight them. The occasional comber has broken right across
the top of the cabin, solid green water that has spurted into
the cabin through the hatchway and also, unfortunately,
through the Tannoy ventilator immediately above my bunk.
I have had the Calor gas heater on to dry out things, and the
sun has begun to shine overhead and its warmth through the
cabin windows is helping to dry out. The motion is quite
comfortable, especially as the wind is now blowing a steady
30 knots, though it sometimes hits the 40 knot mark.

"I have been snoozing until midday if you call a nightmare of shipwreck and disaster a snooze. I have had to go on deck to tie down the storm jib more securely and rescue the steering blade, which fell out of its slot and was floating astern attached by its Terylene line.

"The seas outside are tremendous — crenellated white caps from horizon to horizon, as though you are looking at a crazy city of turretted roofs topped with snow. Seas are about 20 feet high — about twice the height of the coach roof. No question of being able to start sailing in these seas and conditions — absolutely impossible, even for the big monos. I hope I'm not the only poor bastard copping it out here."

Having passed over Leslie Williams, the eye of the storm apparently moved north-east towards Noel Bevan in *Myth of Malham*. This is what Noel wrote in his logbook on Tuesday 11th June —

"0200   Wind up to S.S.W. force 8. Set storm jib. 10 rolls in main.

0400   Wind up to force 9+. Lowered main, reaching under storm jib at 9 knots. Barograph falling 2/10 in. per hour.

0700   Worse. Going right into depression, if goes down to force 8 will be delighted, think 10 now. Anemometer off stop. Hope self-steering holds. Running N.E. at 9 knots.

0730   Definitely force 10. Lowered storm jib and laid ahull.

0900   Still lying beam on. O.K. apart from occasional wave breaking over everything — heeling at 45°–50° and going forward at 1 knot.

1100   Force 10 with horizontal sleet. No visibility at all. Barograph stopped falling. Anemometer on stop at force 10.

1400   Barograph going up. Sun appeared. Still force 9 with veer to the west.

1800   Moderated slightly.

1900   Down to force 7. Set storm jib and 10 rolls in main. Good to be under way again."

The eye of the storm passed directly over *Spirit of Cutty Sark* and *Myth of Malham*, which meant that the main body of the fleet was left to the south of it. The unexpected force is explained by the fact that whereas the weather chart showed the centre 992 millibars, the barometer on *Spirit of Cutty Sark* was reduced to 982 millibars. Presuming that Leslie's barometer was correctly adjusted, the lower pressure would mean a steeper isobaric gradient, with correspondingly stronger winds.

If the storm centre was moving north-east at more than 60 knots, the isobaric gradient will have eased behind the centre as it opened its distance from the high pressure ridge which had shot out across the Atlantic from Nova Scotia. This would explain why Bruce Dalling had a very rough time at dawn, while Noel Bevan was less troubled at midday.

The easing of the isobaric gradient does not, on the other hand, completely explain why Noel had an easier time than Leslie — Leslie was not expecting the storm, and was caught by it. Noel had *Myth of Malham* prepared ahead of the worst that came over him — it is easier to do this in daylight. This is how Noel later amplified the notes in his log — "I was reaching away from it under the little storm jib (80 square feet.) This was too much for her, so I turned and ran with it. All the time it still veered, and I finished up running north-east. I was certainly doing over 10 knots. Then I thought the self-steering gear would carry away because every now and then she would give a little broach and the self-steering gear would slam over to bring her back. The storm jib would jibe over, and this practically pulled the top of the mast off. She obviously couldn't do this — I let her come up under the self-steering gear until she lay broadside on, and then let the sheet go and got the sail down. That was frightening, it crackled — and it was only a tiny sail. It was down very quickly and then she lay ahull, laid over at about 45° under the windage of the mast. She was very comfortable like that, she just stayed like that and went up and down. Every now and then a wave would break on the deck, but not terribly badly."

Bill Howell must have been passed closely by the centre of the storm; Martin Minter-Kemp in *Gancia Girl* was probably some 150 miles south-east from its nearest point as it passed.

It might be thought that this race would attract men of brawn rather than brain because the primary need would be for obstinate, physical endurance, but the need is more for the wisdom of the bamboo bending to the wind than the oak which stands stoutly upright and may be broken. Martin Minter-Kemp has a mild, courteous manner; he peers through spectacles, but the eyes are wise, and the mind has stamina. It is the upbringing and integrity of the "old school tie."

"My father was a soldier, and after the war he was sent to Germany in the occupation forces. I went with him, and was sent to school at Wilhelmshaven on the north German coast. This was where I really learned to sail. The school was run by the occupation forces for the sons of people stationed in Germany, on Navy lines. So I was very fortunate in being able to sail the Naval R.N.S.A. dinghies and bigger yachts quite early on. I think this helps enormously later in life."

Martin first became aware that the storm was at hand while listening to Bill spinning a good yarn for the benefit of the Press, saying that the seas were as big as houses (this was the 10th June front which mysteriously faded.) "I could see from my cabin that the wind was never more than force 3 or 4, and the sea was moderate, but by 0200 on 11th June it was quite obvious that Bill had not been exaggerating. The seas were very large indeed, and in fact I took off all sail, lifted my boards to three-quarters, and lashed the helm. I went below, shut the door, and turned in. I stayed turned in until about 1000 when the seas were awe-inspiring; I was trying to give an accurate estimate of wave height — I think 35 feet would not be overstating the case.

"We stayed like that all day. She lay at about 55° to 60° to the wind very happily indeed. A trimaran, when all sail is down, is just like a Kon-Tiki raft — she bobs around quite happily and settles down on her own to the attitude best suited to the wind. The motion was lively but not violent, and a pot of lime marmalade I had on the shelf did not move at all during the gale.

"Towards nightfall I realised that I was being blown east rather than just north, and that I must do something. At 2130 I reset the mizzen and was able to make a bit of westing, steering perhaps 330° at 4–5 knots. By midnight I was able to put up a spitfire (small jib) and come a little closer to the wind. By the following morning it was all plain sail again."

Brian Cooke, north of Martin, was much closer to the passage of the storm centre — perhaps as close as Bill Howell.

Brian was 47; he had been in banking for 26 years. He sailed with the blessing of Westminster Bank — his participation would obviously give a good image for the men who work the other side of the counter. This official support was wisely placed because Brian had risen to First Mate with the British India Steam Navigation Company during the war. His approach to the race was a blend of the trained seaman and the invincibly methodical banker!

When the wind was close to gale force on the 11th he commented, "Must get the main off her or we will lose it or the mast and we don't want that." The main was securely lashed by 0930. His log entries continue —

"1000   Bar. 1000. Blowing force 9–have never been in such a blow–the small working foresail is up and pulling us along at between 4 and 8 knots, almost running before it.

1100   Bar. 1000. Wind is down to force 8 — what a scream and noise it has all been, even below with all the wash-boards up and the hatch closed.

1200   Bar. 999. Wind 7 to 8–took some photos, wind-speed indicator registering 30 to 38 knots–it has been stronger though. The seas are not so dangerous now. So we are broad-reaching under foresail on 310° so as to make a bit of westing instead of northing. It is wetter than ever below. I am soaked right through. It happened on the foredeck when a wave engulfed me completely — fortunately I was on the weather side of the mast which stopped me going right across to the lee scuppers, perhaps injuring myself in the process. I was secured to the weather rail with my life-line of course. As soon as is prudent I shall close reach under foresail to make more westing. The gale is a repetition of yesterday's, only much stronger — I hope it is not to be a daily occurrence! The sun is out now which makes things much more bearable, but it is still blowing great guns although I think it is moderating all the time. When not over-canvassed, as I had her earlier on I regret to say, she looks after herself without any fuss at all and gives no anxiety.

1315   Wind force 9–as strong or stronger than ever–a positive shriek everywhere. Have just had lunch — stewed steak and potatoes. That should keep me going. Had to put a light lashing on the wind vane retaining split pin just now as it was working out. The gear is working admirably. Have done all I can for the yacht and myself so will lie down and try to relax.

1430   Knock down–yacht fell on her side–probably about 20 feet off the top of a breaker. I was showered on my bunk with the contents of the windward one and the chart table received much of the crockery direct. Otherwise not excessive water inside–soon pumped out–10 minutes at most. On deck, things suffered more. Starboard cockpit dodger ripped clean away at foot and lifebuoy gone adrift — nothing serious that I can see though, i.e., structurally or sailwise. Can't do anything about it at the moment. The sun has been out for some time and the seas are an awe-inspiring sight. Bar. 1000, steady.

1520   Top of a big breaker came aboard on port side (windward.) I was in the hatchway and saw it coming — it carried away half the port dodger. All is well aboard apart from superficial damage mentioned above although the electrics have had a good dunking. The radio has escaped most being that much further from the hatch. Must be blowing force 9.

1540   Overcast and driving rain. Bar. 1,000. We are heading about north-north-west. I'm glad I'm not in one of those cats just now!! The noise is awful in this gale. I have confidence in the yacht's ability to look after me providing I handle her properly which I consider I have done and I am not at all frightened but am extremely respectful and awe-inspired with what these conditions could do in a trice if the yacht were not handled properly. I wonder how local this blow is — it will be interesting to compare notes."

Brian wrote on while the storm continued. At 1930 there was still "little change in the weather, but if anything more moderate. The huge seas seem to have gone down." At 2145 — "Have just had supper–lamb stew and vegetable soup thrown in to one–feel much better for it as I was getting cold — have been soaking wet for 36 hours now — no, 48 hours. Light is going now. Barometer 1004. Must just wait for the wind to subside — cannot do any of the necessary chores below in this weather. Writing even is a great effort. Only thing to do is to lie down."

Jean Yves Terlain also suffered a knock-down in *Maguelonne*. He had lowered his mainsail, and was making 6 knots under storm jib alone. The bow paid off at the top of what was apparently an orbital wave, and the boat was rolled over. Jean Yves was concussed inside his cabin; a large bank of batteries in the forecabin broke loose, damaging the deckhead with the impact and splashing acid over the glassfibre of his hull. The boat was not over for long, but the mess was more of a problem than aboard *Opus*.

Bertrand de Castelbajac took the storm easily; he had been in much worse weather in the English Channel in April when *Maxine*, with no sail set, had leaned over sideways from the wind until the sea was washing around in the cockpit. On the 11th he simply recorded a "force 9 wind between 0900 and 1500." *Maxine* was making excellent progress during this period of the race, drawing ahead of *Dogwatch* and *Rob Roy*, and catching up on the larger boats ahead.

How well had these boats been handled through the storm? So easy to be wise after the event! One can look at the charted tracks and suggest how each boat could have avoided the worst of the trouble and even kept sailing *if given a day's warning of what was coming*.

It was the job of the computer directing Geoffrey Williams to calculate his courses 24 hours ahead, allowing for the weather. He had been sent north, and on the 11th he was sublimely oblivious of all the commotion south of him. It was shortly after the race that Ian Slater, in charge of the computer, wrote an article in *Spectrum* in which he said, "At this stage Williams gained a lead of some 300 miles over his nearest rivals." Later he was more cautious about the mileage gained, but in Newport Geoffrey Williams said, "I think I made up perhaps 200 or 300 miles on *Golden Cockerel* and on *Spirit of Cutty Sark* at this time." The later caution seems right, but undoubtedly Tuesday 11th June was the crucial day that put *Sir Thomas Lipton* into the lead half way through the race because Geoffrey, alone from his rivals, escaped the storm.

8 The rest were caught

9-15 June

Once a yacht has been efficiently brought to rest in a gale, hove to or lying ahull, it can be surprisingly comfortable below in the cabin, and the man who has mastered this art is more like the squatting hedgehog than the harried mouse! As long as the conditions of wind and sea remain reasonably constant, there should be no call to dress in oilskins to clamber out into the weather. One even feels reluctant to start sailing again as the wind begins to drop — it is much easier to justify a long, refreshing sleep.

Bill Howell gives an excellent, detailed description of getting under way, after some 34 hours at rest, on Wednesday 12th June.

"1200 — I have just got the yacht (*Golden Cockerel*) sailing again after clearing up and repairing the storm damage. The gale slowly subsided into a force 6 by midnight, but it was obviously impossible to do all the jobs that had to be fixed, in the dark. So I just snuggled into my bunk, and with the *Cockerel* hove to under reefed mizzen still, I had the first care ree sleep since leaving Plymouth.

"At 0700 I got up to repair the damage.

"First of all I had breakfast — cornflakes, three boiled eggs and coffee. Then there was the revolting job of emptying the bucket, which had the excrement of the gale in it; I had been unable to ditch it over side. The contents of that bucket almost made me sick — I had to hold my breath as I carried it into the cockpit. The next job was to unreel the genoa sheets. They were snarled into a solid bunch and one end-whipping had come off. It took an hour's patient puzzling before I had two neat coils of rope lying in the cockpit.

"Then the bilges. The forward collision bilges had not been emptied for days, because of the weather conditions. The

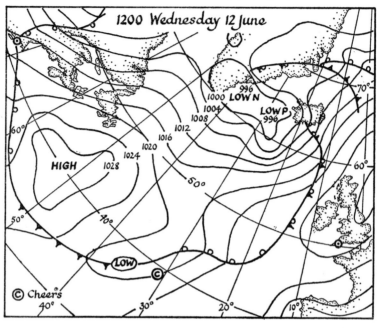

1200 Wednesday 12 June

70°

996
1000 LOW N
1004
LOW P
1008 996
1012
1016
1020
HIGH 1024
1028 60°
50°

50°

40°

LOW
©

© Cheers
40° 30° 20° 10°

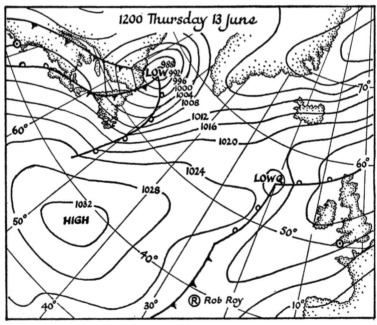

1200 Thursday 13 June

988
LOW 992
996 70°
1000
1004
1008
1012
1016
1020 60°

1024 LOW Q

1028
1032 50°
HIGH 50°

40°

40° 30° ℞ Rob Roy 10°

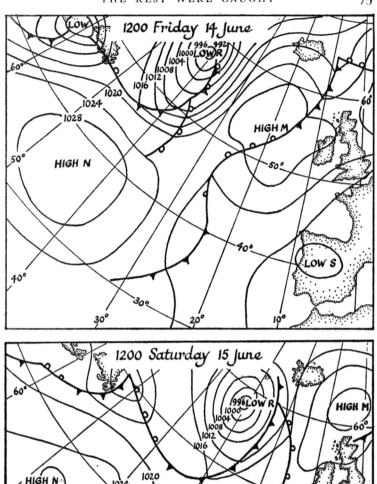

1200 Friday 14 June

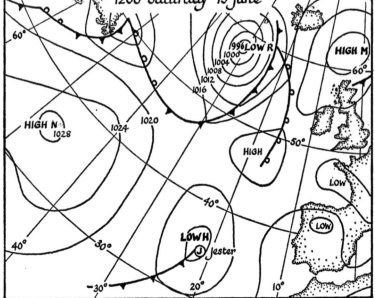

1200 Saturday 15 June

port compartment, which had been to windward with most of the seas washing over it, had almost 2 feet of water in it — the starboard about a foot. I cleared them surprisingly quickly with the dinghy pump. Then I sponged out the port and starboard bilges in the hull, and freed the limber holes. The port hull seems to collect more than the starboard — must be from the rudder gland. The starboard hull certainly seems better since I have stopped using the toilet with its cocks.

"With the bilges clear, I heaved the water tanks and heavy sail bags that I had stowed in the port hull, which was to weather in the storm, back to their allotted places in the starboard hull. The sun broke through a hole in the cloud bank overhead, so I took a quick sunsight — not a very good horizon in the conditions, but it will give me some idea of my longitude I hope. My DR is very hazy — I was simply battling for survival in that storm.

"Then the storm jib was stowed — it had been left lashed to the forestay with ten sail ties to keep it from taking off in the 50 knot wind: I decided to leave its sheets in position — they have their own dead eye leads, and do not get in the way of other sheet leads.

"Then the longest and most important job of all — the self-steering gear. I found that the screws holding the cheeks of the lead together were working loose and had to be re-fastened. The locking nut holding the nut for the main spindle onto which the steering blade slides had worked itself off, and the main nut was working off. God knows how — the thread is badly burred, and I had a hell of a job tightening down the nut. But I haven't another locking nut on board, so this must be checked now, every day. If I lose that spindle, the self-steering will be *kaput*. The wires holding the patent release had begun to fray through — one had only two strands holding it. I served this wire with Terylene cord — I do not think it is dangerous, because it should work on one wire, even if the other frays through. I also tied extra shock cord around the latch gears — I think this is just a futile gesture, as in heavy winds and seas the vane will simply ride out of its worm gear as it did when I was running before the storm. The steering blade was shipped back, and the steering lines to the rudder quadrants reset and greased, the steering wires below deck re-checked, and the gear shipped back in the water. It seems to be working okay again.

"Then the reefs were shaken out of the main and mizzen and the battens, which had taken so much sweat and blood to ease out in the storm, slipped easily back. The mizzen was stowed on its boom, the main and No. 3 genoa raised, and we were off again, hard on a 15 knot south-west wind.

"To complete the morning's work, I recharged both banks of batteries, 12-volt and 24-volt — it has been out of the question trying to use the Honda generator over the last couple of days. I also washed up the dishes and hucked out the cabin.

"Then, at 1100, we began sailing again, and I was back in the race, after those big monos must have stolen a march on me."

Two hours later Bill was hoisting light weather sails in the characteristic calm after gale. At sea, it seems as though the passing violence sucks the wind briefly out of its wake.

Two days earlier a genuine calm had begun to establish itself over the Azores route boats: the Azores High was ridging out towards England, and this meant that the risk most dreaded in taking this southern route was materialising. The famous Voss was becalmed for 22 days in these waters when the Azores High settled over him.

The sky cleared above Tom Follett at 1630 on Monday 10th June. The barometer was rising, and by 1830 he found himself sailing to a fading westerly breeze. This was precisely the expected start for it, and next morning the sun should have turned to brass, banishing virtually all movement from the air. Already lagging behind the boats to the north, Tom's position in the race would have become hopeless. But he was quickly "let off the hook" — by 2300 he was "sailing well with 12–15 knots (force 4) from the west-south-west." A front from the centre of the brewing storm was strong enough to affect his weather long before it arrived over him.

One expects a front to curve discreetly around the solid strength of an established High, but this was no normal front: it set itself against the Azores High like a bull with its head down and forced its way slowly and surely south-eastwards. Already, that evening, it had backed and increased the wind flowing over Tom Follett and he set his course to skirt the northern edge of the Azores Group.

Nigel Burgess had much the same experience, a little later as one would expect. At 0200 on Tuesday 11th June he wrote, "Speed 1 knot. Becoming calm. No. 1 genoa down — up ghoster." Next morning he added, "I made a boob last night and slept through from 0300 to 0900 without waking. When I did we had tacked (or jibed) and everything was aback." By 1345, however, he had changed first to his No. 1 genoa, and then down again to his No. 2 — "Going well. Speed 4 knots. A lovely day. Am now in swimming trunks and oilskin jacket." That evening he wrote, "I hope to hell there are no more calms."

I was too far south and east to share the good fortune of Tom and Nigel. The wind faltered into a calm at 1115 on the 11th while Nigel was picking up speed again, and I was then wallowing for 20 hours. There was often the tantalising suggestion of a light air ruffling over the swell, but if it meant anything it never reached *Rob Roy*. I trimmed the sails and the vaned steering this way and that while futile rage alternated with petty depression.

I had not realized before the race how firmly the emotions can be caught up in the weather — especially when the wind fails, for then one rolls haphazardly in the middle of an airless desert that mesmerizes the mind; one becomes convinced that nothing will break the spell. I looked at the chart again and again: 150 miles to the nearest island in the Azores — I knew it was going to take a week to ten days to reach it. Without doubt, the Azores High had taken up its wonted position to the south of the island group, and there were 500 miles of calm sea ahead of me. It was inevitable; I had been idiotic to attempt this route. "We're in for a slow crossing," I informed my tape recorder — "tomorrow I will look up in the *Pilot* to see which of the islands it might be best to go to for stores (water in particular) — we need a pit stop as we dash round this circuit."

I was granted one small insight during the day when I looked at the word 'becalmed' in my log, and it read like a complaint to the Almighty. Thereafter I wrote 'calm' — it seemed more a statement of fact, and acceptance (and, to course, the mind learns to accept the calms without over much emotional involvement, after the first shock of being bowled over).

After a day of drifting more or less on course, achieved only by constant attention, the soft nightfall found me ready to resign from the effort of sailing. No boob on my part — it was quite deliberate! The barometer was still rising, and the next day would have to start a new routine — I meant to rest before it began.

I was up at first light for breakfast, and at 0630 began to fix the gear for rowing. It would obviously be tiring with the rolling of the boat, but I stowed all sail and bent my weight to the oars to see how long the first trick would last. Within 20 minutes a slight but clear breeze had arrived from the south-south-east! Now I felt more of an idiot than ever: why had I not rowed the day before if the results were so immediate? It also felt as though ten tons of brass weight of the sun had been lifted from the boat — I sprang to hoist the spinnaker, mainsail, mizzen staysail and mizzen, and then stow the oars with their gear.

The wind did not come up to expectations; after 8 hours working with what there was, I had my customary afternoon nap. If premonition woke me early, I ignored it and lay back for a further 15 minutes — all seemed quiet, and if *Rob Roy* was not sailing properly she would bear with me a little longer.

Then, as I emerged into the cockpit, I found myself looking up at the towering bridge of an ocean tug which had just arrived. I scuttled below again for trousers. My mind began to clear — "Switch on the transmitter," I thought, but the receiver made a crackling din: the generator was at work in the cockpit, charging the batteries. I grabbed the flags Mike, India, November (as a three-letter group they make the request to be reported to Lloyds of London.) No time to hoist them–no wind to blow them–I clipped them together and waved them pathetically over the side nearest the tug. This, too, was doomed to futility as a loud hailer boomed from the bridge — "Are you the *Rob Roy?*" My left hand wobbled the flags while my right thumb went up in the air. "Do you

wish to be reported to Lloyds?" — the right thumb went
higher still.

As the flags came inboard, I saw for the first time that the
sails were aback. All hands seemed to be lounging on the side
of the *Britonia*, grinning, waving and taking photographs.
How ridiculous I must have looked! Still dashing to do everything, I put the tiller hard over — but nothing happened,
and nor it could with a collapsed spinnaker in front. I raced
forward and dropped the spinnaker untidily, intending to
hoist a jib in its place. Half way through I had a better idea,
and set about rigging one oar. All the time the *Britonia* was
circling, and all the time the crew was grinning — I did not
dare look at them.

Eventually the oar was pushing the bows round, and one
by one the sails were filled, including the re-hoisted spinnaker.
When she looked a proper ship again, I turned to the *Britonia*
to give a nonchalant wave as much as to say, "There! I can
sail this boat after all, you see—*now* you can take the photographs." The *Britonia* was fast disappearing towards the
horizon, with no one in sight. The moral is clear: do not get
caught with your trousers down.

The south-south-east wind had reached Tom Follett earlier
that morning–at 0430–after a night of patchy calms. The
front from the storm was nearly upon him, and the south-
south-east wind was presumably the drawing of air into the
front (or a local depression formed on it.) By 0500 it was force 5
with rain; by 0615 Tom was in a full gale. For several hours
the wind was then fluky, gusting up from nothing to force 6
and between south-south-east and south-south-west while he
was swept by intermittent rain showers.

At 1000 it seemed settled again at a steady force 8 from
south-south-east with a hazy sun appearing now and then —
at 1025 there was a sudden wind shift to north in torrential
rain. Tom dropped all sail "to await developments. Very odd
weather today!" Odd indeed — the wind veered to north-
east, throwing up a lumpy sea in continuous rain, and by 1400
it was blowing force 10. He was drifting under bare poles some
20 miles south of Flores (he must have passed closely north of
Graciosa the day before, but did not sight the island in poor

Myth of Malham taken through the periscope of U.S. submarine *Hardhead*.

Coila taken from a U.S. aircraft as the paramedics climb aboard.

How ridiculous that two days before I had thought of putting in to Delgada, the other side of the island, to replenish my stores!

To be honest, I was not really enjoying the rum — the cigar even less as I had not smoked since leaving England. Suddenly the wind left me — my contentment vanished. "*You fool!*" I exploded, tossing the cigar to the sea — "How did you dare relax and congratulate yourself? Idiot — you're in the lee of the island." I tried to reason: it did seem bad luck to be blanketed from the wind 11 miles off the island, but fury prevailed — "You will damned well row northwards – all night if need be–till you pick that wind up again." The 'other me' sighed, "The party's over" — and then in the gloaming I rigged the oars, stripped off my sweater and settled down to it with the odd "burp" from the rum. I left the ghosting genoa up with the mainsail and mizzen to fill to the wind as soon as it came. The main boom was raised on the topping lift — underneath I stood, rowing my rage away.

After half an hour a draught from the north whispered to me. I stood bolt upright. No mistaking it, cold and sinister. The sails filled to the port tack as the oars left my hands to trail in the outriggers. The voice of fury was hushed and contrite: nothing to do with the lee of the island; instead, the lull before a shift of wind — but much more, my instincts were aroused and alarmed: if ever the generations of seamen in my family have spoken to me, it was now; galvanised into action — so much to be done.

The main topping lift uncleated, the boom dropped to the sail. Recleat the topping lift — no job to be half done in the gathering dark and wind. The ghosting genoa down–I stood still a moment–we were lying well to the wind under mainsail and mizzen. Now to secure on deck. First the life-raft–pushed forward for the rowing–was replaced on its chocks and securely lashed. Then to lift each oar forwards, back over the stern, and forwards down the companionway — quite safe, loose below. A tommy bar for the strong screws of the outriggers–slow work–but once free, thrown quickly below on a bunk. The wind was increasing — the dark growing. I unhanked the ghosting genoa, bundled it down the forehatch, unshackled the sheets from the clew, and closed the forehatch. Then down the

Myth of Malham taken through the periscope of U.S. submarine *Hardhead*.

Coila taken from a U.S. aircraft as the paramedics climb aboard.

Cheers.   *Photo: Fotografix Inc.*

visibility.)

At 1830 Tom hoisted his foresail — the north-east wind had dropped to force 8; his barometer was now rising again.

That evening at 2110 Nigel Burgess wrote, "have just heard over the radio (Radio Canada) that Leslie Williams reckons he is in force 12, 1,100 miles from Plymouth. I hope they are all O.K." That was Nigel's last entry for nearly three days. At noon on Saturday 15th June he wrote that he was 75 miles from Corvo Rock.

As I have said, the front was moving slowly; 24 hours after it passed Tom Follett, I was still oblivious of its approach. At 1237 on Saturday 13th June I sighted the cloud cap over Santo Miguel, 36 miles ahead. The wind was backing slowly from south-south-east to south-south-west — as force 3–4 since 1030, it was giving the first easy sailing for seven days. At 1415 below the cloud, Pointa do Arnel appeared as a left hand edge to the island.

Santo Miguel is the largest island in the Azores group; its bulk was looming faintly through a mist which was firmly hiding the top of the nearest mountain, the Pico da Vara, 3,623 feet high. By 1900, however, the peak had cleared into view; I took a vertical sextant angle of 2°35′ which converted to a range of 12.9 miles through Lecky's tables — this combined with a compass bearing of 232° gave a fix 2 miles south of the dead reckoning which I had plotted on from the position of a third sunsight at 1005. As the gentle set of the prevailing current was southerly, I felt happy with what seemed a faultless landfall. I had hoped to reach this point in ten days rather than 12, but after the calms of the past week I was well content.

Celebration was clearly proper: a special dinner of chicken curry followed by loganberries. Then I broke my rule about spirits for a rum and coke; I even lit a cigar. I leaned back comfortably in the cockpit and gazed with appreciation at the island.

In the evening light the houses were beginning to twinkle their positions, and I tried to imagine the people inside. After 12 days of ocean, the deep green of Santo Miguel was enchanting and, as it is 35 miles long, I could hope to gaze at it again happily over my breakfast.

How ridiculous that two days before I had thought of putting in to Delgada, the other side of the island, to replenish my stores!

To be honest, I was not really enjoying the rum — the cigar even less as I had not smoked since leaving England. Suddenly the wind left me — my contentment vanished. "*You fool!*" I exploded, tossing the cigar to the sea — "How did you dare relax and congratulate yourself? Idiot — you're in the lee of the island." I tried to reason: it did seem bad luck to be blanketed from the wind 11 miles off the island, but fury prevailed — "You will damned well row northwards – all night if need be–till you pick that wind up again." The 'other me' sighed, "The party's over" — and then in the gloaming I rigged the oars, stripped off my sweater and settled down to it with the odd "burp" from the rum. I left the ghosting genoa up with the mainsail and mizzen to fill to the wind as soon as it came. The main boom was raised on the topping lift — underneath I stood, rowing my rage away.

After half an hour a draught from the north whispered to me. I stood bolt upright. No mistaking it, cold and sinister. The sails filled to the port tack as the oars left my hands to trail in the outriggers. The voice of fury was hushed and contrite: nothing to do with the lee of the island; instead, the lull before a shift of wind — but much more, my instincts were aroused and alarmed: if ever the generations of seamen in my family have spoken to me, it was now; galvanised into action — so much to be done.

The main topping lift uncleated, the boom dropped to the sail. Recleat the topping lift — no job to be half done in the gathering dark and wind. The ghosting genoa down–I stood still a moment–we were lying well to the wind under mainsail and mizzen. Now to secure on deck. First the life-raft–pushed forward for the rowing–was replaced on its chocks and securely lashed. Then to lift each oar forwards, back over the stern, and forwards down the companionway — quite safe, loose below. A tommy bar for the strong screws of the outriggers–slow work– but once free, thrown quickly below on a bunk. The wind was increasing — the dark growing. I unhanked the ghosting genoa, bundled it down the forehatch, unshackled the sheets from the clew, and closed the forehatch. Then down the companionway and up for'd–near dark below–to haul out the working jib stowed in its bag, and lug it back to the foredeck. The neck of the bag untied, the tack of the sail was snapped to its pendant on the stem. Then the bag drawn back from the sail was stuffed through the forehatch onto the ghosting genoa. Now the piston hanks were one by one snapped to the forestay, the foot of the sail drawn aft and the sheets shackled to the clew. The lead of the sheets was wrong for the smaller sail: I went back to the cockpit for pliers, the block slides to be pushed forwards in their tracks, screwed down again and tightened. On the port side a seizing wire had been chafed off the shackle securing the sheet block to its slide–must be replaced, now, I thought–I sat on the deck, the torch and pliers between my legs dangling over the windward side. The pin of the shackle bound, I hoisted the working jib–she heeled hard–I dropped the mainsail and lashed it to its boom.

Then below for oilskins and seaboots; some 20 minutes had passed — I was ready.

As I came up to stand in the cockpit, the full force of the squall struck. The wind and rain lashed us over, water cascading off the sails; but there was nothing more to do now than see how she settled.

I switched on the compass light and watched the heading carefully — moving either side of 030°; on the safe tack, we were standing out to the open sea. I went below, put a towel along the near edge of the chart table to absorb my dripping, and laid off the opposite tack. The 35 miles of Santo Miguel were now a lee shore, but our present heading was back towards England. The starboard tack looked safe on the chart–just diverging from the shore–so I went back to the cockpit and put *Rob Roy* about. She settled with the compass reading 285°–290° — allowing for a variation of 16°45′ W we were heading just north of west.

After a while I became bored as *Rob Roy* no longer needed me. Is it intuition or indolence that tells the singlehander to go below to his bunk? A long yawn decided to leave the question waiting–but not the bunk–and I slept peacefully for nearly 3 hours.

I woke to a clearance and took bearings of the Pointa do Cintrao light and the right hand edge of the island — a rough fix, but it seemed to confirm the heading as just north of west. I lay down again; we had covered two-thirds of the island, but I did not settle in sleep this time. Within an hour the wind was backing, and in the light of dawn it became clear that we were sliding in to the end of the island. The wind was also dropping; I hoisted the mainsail to sail more tightly to the wind — we left the western end of Santo Miguel a little over 3 miles to port.

During the five days 9th–14th June Michael Richey was rapidly progressing southwards towards the trade wind belt. Then in the evening of the 14th he came to a halt.

"2100 — No wind at all; the sea like a desert with a slow rolling swell from the north-east. The side hatches are off. For lunch: an onion and two carrots, biscuits, Cheddar, too much wine. The wine is interesting. Every flagon tastes different and each flagon tastes different every day. The present one tastes like coloured water.

"15 June — 34°42′N 21°27′W (noon) — I must have dozed off without meaning to last night. In any event, *Jester* was lying with no wind at all; but at about 0500 this morning I woke to find her sailing along quite nicely, at about 4 knots I reckoned. I roused myself to check the course, to find that it was due east. There was no indication, of course, of how long she had been on this heading, but we had probably made some 20 miles since midnight. The wind was now from the south, in an area where the Pilot charts indicate the extreme improbability of any but northerly winds. I put *Jester* on a westerly course and turned in again, to dream of telling Francis (Sir Francis Chichester) despairingly about all this. 'Why don't you learn how to sail her to windward?' he asked, 'I should drop in at the Museo Naval in Madrid — they will teach you how.'

"At about 0800 I lay in my bunk — frustrated and angry. This finally meant that I could scarcely make the passage in under 50 days, and I was by no means sure that I had food and water enough for longer. I refused to get up, but lay smouldering at the perversity of circumstances. I must have dozed off, because the sound of wind brought me to my feet just in time. We had been hit by a line squall, and within a couple of minutes the heavens had opened and the wind had risen to gale force. The torrents of rain cut the visibility down to a few yards, and above I could see an evil black cloud, apparently on the point of disintegration. I got all the sail off and stowed neatly, just in time. I could not turn her head to wind to lower and the yard and top batten came down outside the topping lift. I clambered onto the coach roof, and with some difficulty got them the right side — a hairy operation. Finally, there she lay; and as far as I was concerned it could blow as hard as it liked, and from whatever quarter because I had hundreds of miles of sea room. The cold front spent the rest of the day getting through, but the strong blow lasted only about a quarter of an hour. In the evening I passed through the eye of the low — it must have been a small one: ominous walls of precipitating cloud seemed to surround the centre where there was no wind and a nasty, confused sea. Finally, the whole system passed by, and a blue band on the horizon grew wider and wider, and then one could see low cumulus cloud in it, caught by the setting sun."

So passed the front which had an arm as long as the Law. The weather charts were showing its progress southwards each day; a small depression developed the day it passed over Tom Follett — another is shown over Michael Richey on the 15th.

Ambrima, sailed by the Frenchman, Marc Cuiklinski, was dismasted on the 12th and her rudder apparently torn off, damaging the transom. She was taken in tow by a Spanish vessel, but sank while nearing the Spanish coast.

Gunthur III had been having trouble with a maststep fitting since before the race. Guy Piazzini sailed her into Plymouth on the 13th, and retired on the 16th.

Sir Alec Rose was sailing northwards at this time, nearing the end of his celebrated circumnavigation. The force of the front had been strong enough to reach down, somewhat attenuated, to his position several hundred miles south-west of Flores — "We had very light wind, calm sea and a clear sky, with bright, moonlit nights until the 12th, when it blew up strongly from the north-east. Black, low clouds scudded by and there was a whine in the rigging. It was much cooler and I had a woollen jersey on. Quite a sea got up as we headed into it. The wind varied in strength and direction, backing from north-east to north-north-west; right on our nose the whole time. It was a succession of tacks, heading into a lumpy sea, with low cloud and rain and pitch-black nights. Desperately slow progress. On the night of the 14th it blew up to force 7 and I had to turn out in heavy rain to reef the mainsail. By dawn we were becalmed, and lay for a whole 24 hours, wallowing in a lumpy sea, with misty rain."

His description of the weather fits my own experience quite closely — at the time I was the nearest to him. His strong wind of the night of the 14th was blowing over *Rob Roy* towards him the day before, but whereas he had to beat into it, for me it was a convenient beam wind. *Rob Roy* was sailing under working jib only, breasting the towering, tumbling seas. Inclined to be a miser with wind estimates, I was prepared to admit to force 8 gusts. At 1655 I sighted Pico, 7,613 feet high, 80 miles to the north-west. The wind at the top of the peak looked mighty: ripping around the great rock, it was forming clouds from nowhere and as rapidly dispensing with them — I imagined myself climbing, but felt much safer below in the sea!

9 Half way 15 - 18 June

During the period of the 11th June storm Tom Follett was
making remarkable progress in *Cheers*. Lagging considerably
behind the leaders on the 9th, six days later he was level with
Voortrekker and *Sir Thomas Lipton*, having shot away from
Dogwatch and *Rob Roy* to leave them racing each other. In
particular, during the 24 hours after 1600 on the 13th Tom
logged nearly 250 miles, easily the longest day's run of any
boat in the race.

The design of *Cheers* is a development of the traditional
Pacific Island flying proa. The flying proa is basically a
sailing canoe with an outrigger attached to it which always
remains to windward. As the wind pressure on the sails starts
to heel the proa, lifting the outrigger from the water, the
crew scrambles backwards and forwards to keep the outrigger
nicely flying. When it flies clear of the waves, the drag of the
water is low on the main hull alone; if the outrigger rises too
far, the greater angle of heel reduces the efficiency of the sails—
hence the scrambling athwartships! The flying proa must be
great fun and it probably gives the fastest sailing possible for
a given waterline length, short of rising on hydrofoils.

The designer, Dick Newick, had the brilliant and original
idea of reversing the wind direction for singlehanding. The
photograph of *Cheers* shows the result: the outrigger provides
buoyancy stability to leeward rather than weight stability
to windward. Designing it for buoyancy gave it the same
basic shape (below the sheer line) as the main hull, and this
'twinning' of the hulls has led experts to describe *Cheers* as
nearer the double canoe than the flying proa. She has also
been described as a monohull with outrigger, a catamaran
with the masts on one hull instead of amidships, and as a wide

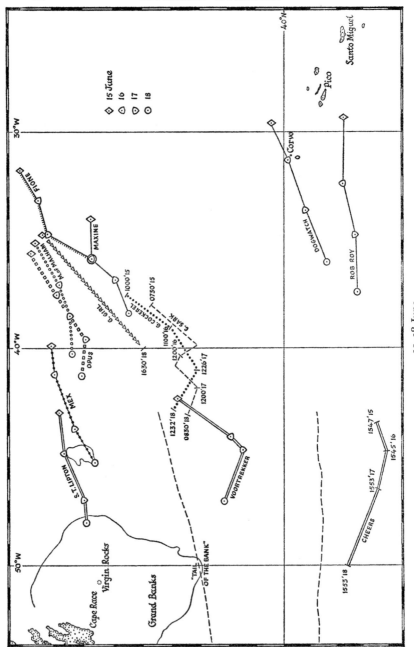

15–18 June

trimaran with one outer hull removed. In fact, with her bright yellow paint, she was nicknamed 'banana split' when launched in the West Indies in the December before the race.

Cheers is nevertheless the same as the flying proa in one important characteristic: she cannot tack — this would bring the wind onto the 'wrong' side. The equivalent of tacking requires a sequence of events which can best be described in terms of the photograph of *Cheers* facing page 81, presuming that one wishes to change direction to sail 'into' the picture instead of 'out of it'. First the jib is lowered, and then the boat is steered out of the wind. The sheets are slackened to let the two Bermudan sails flap (the booms lying across the boat), and then the tiller is disconnected. The dagger board, which is not in sight in the photograph, is then raised, and the one which can be seen in front of the nearer mast is lowered (the two dagger boards are symmetrically opposed outboard of the masts.) When the tiller is connected to the newly lowered board, the endless sheets can be pulled in the 'opposite' direction (bringing the booms out of the picture) and the boat will start sailing into the picture. She can then be steered up into the wind on the new tack, and the jib carried to the other end of the boat to be set flying again on what is now the leading mast. Finally, the newly raised board is adjusted to give directional stability, its tip projecting into the water. As the hulls are now moving in the opposite direction they are of course symmetrically double-ended.

'Roundabouts and swings' — what *Cheers* gains in one capability she is liable to lose in another. Happy with the space of an ocean, she can be very hard to manoeuvre in a crowded anchorage. With greater stability than other multihulls when sailing normally, she will more easily capsize if caught aback. Swift when in her own choice of sailing conditions, she can be slow if she finds the going difficult.

The difficult going which she found on the 15th would, however, have slowed any boat in the race — *Cheers* was sailing straight towards the centre of a High. Luckily for Tom, the High was moving to the east. At 1900 on the 15th the wind was fading away from a northerly direction; during the 16th he barely moved while the High was passing over him; at 0330 on the 17th the wind was building up from the south-

south-west as his position drew away to the west of the centre of the High. He then sailed by far the longest day's run of any boat during this 3 day period of the race. He had left his midway point in the race far behind him and would soon be 1,000 miles from Newport.

At 1000 on the 15th Bill Howell had written, "We are at the half way mark now." It was a day of gentle winds, and at 1700 he wrote, "Transatlantic race forecast: variable 2–4. Fair, moderate, but some fog patches. Well, what do you know? Mildest forecast we have had up to date."

The wind increased after dark and turned against him — "It is amazing how you learn to change sail in the dark. I do not bother turning the cross-tree light on — I use the cabin light alone for illumination. Another advantage of a catamaran."

Another front was approaching him, and at 0600 on the 16th he described it as "a dirty overcast morning. Although it is blowing quite hard, we are in thick sea fog and visibility is down to 50 yards. 15 days of bloody headwinds!! Will they never free!!"

Bill needed the wind to be free to gain on Leslie Williams. The weaving tracks of *Golden Cockerel* and *Spirit of Cutty Sark* during this 3 day period show his determination to hang on, waiting for that free wind which surely must come. The 16th was certainly another difficult day — "What a rough ride! She keeps rearing to the tops of these short, breaking seas and thumping down hard into the hole on the other side. The ride is like going across an Australian paddock in a jeep with four flat tyres. Shifted water and sails into port, windward hull to keep it down." The next day was pleasantly sunny again — "a contrast to yesterday — but as I keep observing, this north Atlantic ocean is an ocean that contrasts weather conditions daily as the depressions speed one after another to the east."

For the 4th day running the wind was heading him southwards, and now he was near the latitude of the 'Tail of the Bank.' The Gulf Stream, as it flows eastwards past the Tail of the Bank, fans out to weaken and be re-named the Atlantic Current. Before reaching the Tail the current is still liable to be strong, and Bill was aiming to keep just north of it by passing closely north of the Tail. He was now sufficiently close to be looking for signs of the Gulf Stream, slowly losing its character — he recorded sightings of sargasso weed, Portuguese men o' war and even a bosun bird with its long forked tail.

At midday on the 17th he went about onto the port tack to sail northwards, and the next morning he was wondering how Leslie Williams was coping — "He must have logically followed my reasoning and gone north. But you can never tell with the Services — they are trained to think differently to normal people!" Bill and Leslie were in fact still side by side, not more than a few horizons from each other, having taken the northerly tack together.

Brian Cooke was apparently at this stage close to Noel Bevan. Brian also had gentle winds or none at all on the 15th, and he shows the generation of his upbringing by describing the calms as "harry flatters."

At 0500 on the 16th — "Got her going at last" and at 1000, "feel virtuous as I've just had a wash (overdue) and a general clean up. I don't find I get very dirty, but extremely salty!" At 1100, "no following wind at all since Plymouth," and he underlined it. At 1330 he was in the fog which had reached Bill early in the morning, and he raised his morale by having "onion soup with dehydrated onion thrown into it to make sure it is the real thing, and then added at the last minute before taking the pan off the stove was a tin of prawns — added at the last minute so they do not lose their flavour. Salted cheese biscuits accompanied by the brew which was delicious."

The rising wind and sea that day did not plague *Opus* as it did *Golden Cockerel* — Brian simply wrote, "Plugging into it and a bit bumpy."

The next day Brian made a comment on his daily routine — "Navigation and other chores always keep me occupied until lunchtime." Then he added — "I was listening to a conversation Bill Howell was having with the *Daily Mail* yesterday, and he said he hadn't had a wash since leaving Plymouth. I thought to myself that he should have done, when I remembered that I hadn't had any more than a face and hands rinse over." Bill in fact made amends the next morning —

"0815 — I have just had my first fresh water wash since the start of the race. I have also changed all my underwear and feel the better for it. I have even tidied up my bunk."

At midday on the 15th Martin Minter-Kemp was quite close to Brian Cooke and Noel Bevan, but during the next 3 days he diverged southwards. Brian and Noel were following Geoffrey Williams towards Cape Race on the Great Circle route. Like Bill and Leslie, Martin was aiming for the Tail of the Bank. About this time he had an incident with a Russian trawler while becalmed — she "came over the horizon and took a lot of photographs of me as she circled me. Finally she came alongside and I thought, 'Well, here's me for the salt mines — another trimaran written off.' In fact they threw a large engine bolt on a piece of string which nearly broke one of my windows, and on the end of the string was a bottle of brandy inside a seaman's very dirty sock. I thought, 'I really can't explain in Russian that I'm not allowed to receive any sort of stores en route–if I do I shall certainly be arrested on the spot'–so I went below and got a small bottle of champagne which I threw back. Honour was satisfied, and they went away singing the Volga Boatsong."

Noel had a meeting with a submarine, on the 13th — "At 1100 *Myth of Malham* was ambling along on a close reach– the wind about force 2 from the north-west–when I heard a diesel close by. Going on deck, I saw a black conventional submarine on the surface, aimed at me and going at high speed.

"I thought he was a Russian — no ensign or number visible, but he rounded up a few yards off and a stars and stripes fluttered abaft the fin.

"A row of heads appeared above and there was the usual call for name, where from and to. They shouted that they had been around me for about two hours, at periscope depth.

"They gave me a position check and took many photographs. They also offered me a time check, but I felt that I could give the check to them with *Myth of Malham's* Golay crystal clock! They could not understand why I had no crew . . .

"Come aboard for a cup of coffee"

"Sorry, I can't really come on board"

"We are dry, but we can give you a cup of coffee"

"Many thanks, but I have got loads of drink on board here —
and besides, the race rules don't allow me to partake of assistance, refreshment, or anything else"

"What race?"

While Noel was patiently explaining, he noticed that there
was no identification showing, so he asked —

"What's your name?"

"Hardhead"

"No — the name of the submarine, not the captain!"

This went down well with the crew. Laughing, it was their
turn to explain — it was the submarine's name which was
Hardhead. The name of the commanding officer was Captain
David B. McClary; they exchanged addresses and, after the
race, wrote to each other.

The *Hardhead* made off at high speed on the surface, and
Noel felt a certain relief — "one always has the worry about
vessels trying to come alongside." In fact the captain of this
submarine had manoeuvred with care and precision —
"a jolly good and thoughtful seaman."

The photograph of *Myth of Malham* facing page 80 was
taken through the periscope of the *Hardhead* before she surfaced.

Sunday the 16th dawned peacefully on *Rob Roy*. After the
tranquil blue and grey of first light, an orange sun rose from
the clear, sharp horizon, its warmth at once reaching *Rob Roy*
along the golden path it played across the sea. The day promised
pure pleasure in the sailing; on course in a force 3 northerly
wind, we were moving swiftly without any fussing by waves.

I took a sunsight at 0718 and another at 0948 — this was
lucky for timing as at 1000 the sun was abruptly obscured.
"I appeared to be affected by the tail remains of fog banks,
quite possibly blown down from the Grand Banks and by
now merely surviving as areas of thick haze." The weather
chart shows that I was in the southern part of a col in which
the two Highs were dominant and funnelling between them
a stream of air eastwards off the Grand Banks, the wind
accelerating in the middle of the col over *Golden Cockerel* and
then curving southwards more slowly to *Rob Roy*.

These hazy banks spoiled the wind as they passed overhead
— it fell light and headed *Rob Roy* from west to north-west.

"In fact this is only the second time on the passage that I have been completely headed by the wind" — this makes an interesting comparison with Bill and Brian writing about their continuous head winds.

"The banks of haze cleared, and by 1700 the northerly wind had reasserted itself at force 6. Then I sighted what I think was an American merchantman. He seemed to be closing me, and as it was now four days since I had been reported I decided to do my utmost to identify myself." I tried in vain to raise him on the transmitter — he was obviously not maintaining a listening watch on 2182 kc/s, the international voice distress frequency.

"As the mizzen was furled, I had the seemingly bright idea of hoisting the three flags, Mike India November, on the mizzen halyard. So I bent them on and up they went; just before they reached the top they blew apart—November fluttered down again, and Mike and India streamed out at the masthead.

In my annoyance I immediately set about trying to climb the mizzen to recover the flags, but by the time I had come aft again with the climbing rope, Mike and India were no longer to be seen — they had blown off completely and gone overboard. I tried to climb the mast to recover the mizzen halyard which was now, of course, stuck at the top, and I learned something new about climbing masts at sea: it is not the rolling of the boat which is difficult, but the pitching. If a boat is pitching violently, this is the motion which really shakes a man as he tries to go aloft."

The higher I went, the fiercer the sudden wrenching of arms and legs each time the bows punched a wave. Simple leverage it may be — the simpler instinct for survival brought me down again long before I could grasp the end of the halyard.

Next morning I shook out six rolls in the mainsail as the northerly wind eased to force 5. Force 4 by midday — I needed the mizzen. I could not muster the slightest enthusiasm, but decided I must climb before relaxing for lunch. The decision made, I quickly went up with determination, and without forethought. My right hand was about to grab the halyard when I suddenly realised that the mast was buckling forwards on the punches of the pitching. Once again a rapid slither down: I had discovered the hard way that my weight might be sufficient to break the mast forwards from the top of the shrouds if I did not rig the masthead backstay first. Third time lucky — but I do maintain that the fastest way of learning seamanship in a yacht is to make "heaps of silly mistakes — without accidents!"

My mind now began brooding because it was the sixth day since the *Britonia* had reported me; worse, I had only raised one ship on my transmitter since leaving Plymouth. Why? The transmitter had a mean range of 250 miles — I was always within that distance of at least one shipping lane. I had spoken to Lands End Radio at 0100 on the 8th at a range of about 700 miles — surely there could be nothing wrong with the transmitter? We had assumed that I would pass a message every other day with no difficulty — my imagination was brewing an obsessional storm, picturing my family with no news.

If an emotion becomes bottled up, the singlehander needs an outlet like conversation. This gives a simple reason for singlehanders chatting to themselves; it is not a splitting of the mind — just keeping it healthy and whole. If you have a mascot to talk to, like Sir Alec Rose and his bear, Algy, it even has an air of respectability. When I felt the need to talk I said my prayers aloud — as this amounted to more than an hour each day, even the atheist will have to admit that it was ample therapy!

One of my Church Councils had generously given me a $\frac{1}{2}$ bottle of champagne to be opened halfway across (another for the finish!) so I named the halfway mark the 'champagne line'. In the afternoon, "After taking three sunsights I realised that we were rapidly approaching the champagne line; I must do my best, as it were, to dress for dinner for the occasion. By a happy coincidence it was also the first evening for some days when conditions were quiet enough on the boat for a jolly good wash." This was one of the luxuries of the Azores route: the washing itself was not enjoyable–it felt like a draughty bed-bath standing up–but when dressed again one tingled and glowed. This time, however, the satisfaction was shortlived.

"I looked at the ship's clock. I should explain that I proudly

keep three times on board. The basic time is of course that of
the chronometer which keeps G.M.T.; the watch on my
wrist keeps the zone time, the actual time to which I am
working (at the moment zone +2) and then the ship's clock
(the alarm clock on the bulkhead) keeps the time at home so
that I can look at it and visualize what the family is doing —
it said 2025, and I realised that Elizabeth would have put the
children to bed, probably have had her supper, and be sitting
down to another empty evening wondering when she would
hear any news.

"My imagination was at work again: 5 year-old Olivia
asleep — her hair flowing over the pillow; Marcus, aged 8,
lying on his back looking at the ceiling — his nose twitching
while his eyes have the steady stare of a good day dream;
Hugh, aged 10, lying on his side — his eyes on a book just a
few inches from his face. Elizabeth downstairs, sitting alone . . .
my shoulders began to shake; I broke down, and with the
tears came the feeling that all point in the race was lost if I was
only causing worry at home because I could not get reports
through of my position and safety."

Once admitted to myself, this longing for my family was
never far from me until my return to Plymouth on Sunday
1st September. I believe it to be the strongest emotion with
which the normal singlehander has to cope (Leslie Williams
wrote in his logbook within 5 hours of the start that he was
already missing his family) — but it is not generally recognised
as it can be so easily forgotten once one is reunited.

I felt as though I had been shallow, taking my family for
granted; the depths of an unknown love now came to the
surface, and I began to understand better the feelings of
St Paul, cut off in prison, when he wrote to his friends saying
that he longed for them from the depths of yearning.

Paradoxically I was content to be alone in *Rob Roy*, mid-
ocean; my imagination was too realistic in visualizing the
family with me — the seasickness, bickering, and anxiety of
someone falling overboard!

How does one explain this paradox of 'longing without
loneliness?' The turmoil in the mind only builds up as the
days go by without a message being passed. Peace of mind
returns as soon as a fresh contact is made to report the chart

Opus with Brian Cooke.   *Photo: Eileen Ramsay*

"Transatlantic Incident" from a painting by Laurence Bagley.

Fione with Bertil Enbom.   *Photo: Eileen Ramsay.*

position, and condition of vessel and crew. Those who have a transmitter powerful enough to reach the shore stations hardly seem to meet the problem; the daily message achieves the feeling of being united with the family. Peace came to me quickly that evening:

"Finally I was ready for the celebration meal and duly opened the bottle of champagne, and then I thought 'Now! one more try on the transmitter.' I was promptly answered by a very foreign and very longwinded voice! He gave me a string of identifications, name and call sign which I barely understood, but the four-letter call sign began with the word 'Papa', so I said, "I shall call you 'Papa'" and Papa I called him! The feeling of gaiety was powerful aboard *Rob Roy* that evening as I drank the champagne from a humble mug. The champagne line in 16 days 20 hours — it seemed possible with prevailing weather ahead to reach Newport in 32 days.

Dogwatch and *Rob Roy* were leaving the Azores on what was theoretically the best leg of their route, the stretch between the longitude of Flores and the entry into the Gulf Stream. *Rob Roy* had started well by moving further westwards during this 3 day period than any other boat as shown on the analysis chart. *Cheers* had nearly reached the longitude of Cape Race; from the chart positions as plotted it appears she was now leading, more than 100 miles nearer the Nantucket Lightvessel than any other boat. *Dogwatch* moved further westward during this 3 day period than any boat shown on the direct route.

Two boats not previously mentioned are on the analysis chart for this chapter. *Mex* is shown behind *Sir Thomas Lipton*, at this point challenging the lead; she is a beautiful and efficient One Ton Cup boat, designed by the American, Dick Carter, and built in Germany where Claus Hehner, her skipper, works as an architect. *Mex* is the nickname of Claus Hehner's wife.

As I can only count to three in German, our conversation on tape after the race was liable to be like this:

"Q. Do you have any particular impressions of the race which you remember?

A. Yes, I had all things twice. Only the pilots of my hand lamp and of my desk lamp, and naturally they are defect."

I wish I was able to say more about Claus Hehner's race.

Fione, sailed by Bertil Enbom, Lieutenant in the Swedish Army, was making a remarkable passage. She and *Goodwin II* were 19.7 feet overall and the smallest ever to sail in the race. Aboard *Fione* was a Swedish copy of the book which David Lewis wrote on the 1960 race, *The Ship would not Travel Due West*; it provides a good track chart of the boats in that race, won by Sir Francis Chichester. "I was very surprised when after a week I found that I was on approximately the same position as Chichester was in the first race, and I supposed that I must have had tremendously good weather. The next week I was about a day behind and I supposed that I was having very, very good weather, but wait and see . . . " On the 18th *Fione* arrived in the chart position left by *Maxine* two days before.

"One of the most dramatic and lucky air-sea rescues of all time" was said of Joan de Kat after *Yaksha* broke up and sank.

An aircraft picked up his S.O.S. at 0730 on Tuesday, 18th. He gave his position as 54°N 30°W; he had lost his rudder, his mast and one hull — unable to stay afloat, he was abandoning ship.

Shackletons at Ballykelly immediately started searching a plotted area of 36,000 square miles — approximately the size of Ireland. Ocean weather ship, *Charlie*, moved to the area, and the *Irish Rowan*, *Alice Bowater*, *Brunseck* and *Empress of England* also joined the search.

As the search area was 600 miles from Ireland, the Shackletons had only 2 hours flying time over the area before returning to base. They do not carry parachutes as they fly too low to use them — aircraft have been lost during similar exercises. One was in serious trouble on the 19th, but it reached Shannon safely, escorted by another aircraft.

On Thursday 20th a crew member spotted the orange dinghy at 1840, 150 miles before reaching the search area — the position was 53°55′N 23°45′W.

Joan de Kat was waving and firing red flares, 215 miles from the position which he gave when abandoning ship.

A Lindholme rescue dinghy was dropped near him with

survival packs containing water, food and cigarettes. Later he was landed in Denmark from a Danish fishing vessel, having been picked up by the Norwegian bulk carrier, *Jagona*.

At 1553 on Tuesday the 18th Tom Follett completed the 24 hour run of nearly 190 miles that gave him a clear lead in the race. He commented, "A bit too far north at the moment."

His course was rapidly converging on the Gulf Stream. The Admiralty Chart 3272 has two pecked lines showing the ordinary limits of the Gulf Stream, and Tom's chart position at 1553 on the 18th was 47 miles from its southern ordinary limit.

These limits on either side of the Stream have been likened to the sides of a valley along which a river meanders: the path of the Gulf Stream meanders inside the two ordinary limits. But whereas a river flows between its banks, the Gulf Stream is water flowing through water — its meanderings are like a hose being trailed along a slippery path, free to change the pattern of its snaking.

The Gulf Stream is pushed out fast from the Carribean Sea, and then gradually loses its momentum. This produces a 'piling up' from behind as though the hose is being *pushed* along the slippery path — it loops out sideways. The loops then break off to form independent eddies or 'rings.' A ring breaking to the left rotates clockwise — to the right, anti-clockwise. Two rings so formed have been plotted for more than six months, the centres moving erratically about 5 miles a day *backwards* against the eastward flow of the Stream, keeping clear of it, and only gradually becoming smaller. At one point the two rings joined together for several days, measuring about 250 miles by about 80.

The behaviour of the Gulf Stream is complicated and, at present, far from fully understood, but one point at least should be clear: in this race we could be quite certain that

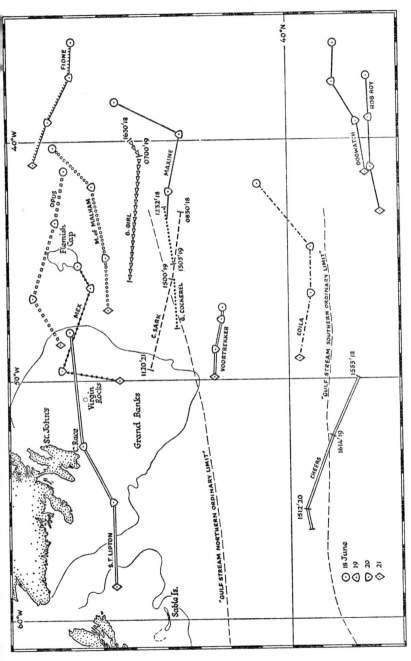

18–21 June

in the general area of the Stream we would be quite uncertain what direction and strength of current we would meet!

After his comment that he was too far north, Tom spent the next 24 hours sailing further north still, against a light westerly wind. He did not hoist his genoa because without it he could head closer to the wind, keeping to the south of the Gulf Stream as much as possible. At the end of this day's run his chart position was only 8 miles south of that pecked line showing the southern ordinary limit.

During the evening of the 19th the wind backed to the south — Tom eased his sheets to sail faster, setting his No. 3 jib. By 0410 the next morning, however, the wind had veered to south-west, and he was close-hauled again while it slowly blew harder. He made a better day's run–escaping the Gulf Stream–but at the end of the run his chart position was 45 miles inside the southern ordinary limit of the Stream, and for some unknown period during the next 48 hours he was badly caught in it.

While this was happening, the wind backed slightly, but then two fronts began to pass over him. It blew up to force 10, and Tom spent about 7 hours under bare poles. At 0815 on the 21st a sudden wind shift to the north-west indicated the passage of the second front, and soon the wind began to moderate.

Some 200 miles north of the Gulf Stream, *Sir Thomas Lipton* was rapidly overhauling *Cheers*, but while Geoffrey Williams was standing in towards the coast of Nova Scotia, in the early hours of the 21st he found himself in trouble. His mizzen staysail halyard had jammed in its block at the masthead. When he tried to climb the mast to cut the sail down he was wrenched off by the pitching of the boat and fell from a height of about 20 feet. No bones were broken; he went to his bunk, badly shaken. At first light he climbed again with wire-cutters–the sail had to come down so that he could tack away from the coast–and this time it was the sail that suddenly fell to the deck. Geoffrey then slept for 4 hours recovering from the considerable shock of this ordeal. Nevertheless, he had whittled away Tom Follett's lead to almost nothing.

Sir Thomas Lipton had already left far behind another problem–icebergs–now facing the boats on the direct route as

Leslie Williams explains: at 0830 on the 18th he was "rushing through fog at 6 knots spurting to 8 — absolutely flat water with a long, long swell of about 4 feet. Quite eerie.

"I listened carefully to the ice reports as I neared the Grand Banks ice zone, and I picked my course to pass just south of the 'southernmost known bergs', the idea being to get safely north of the adverse Gulf Stream current but stay south of the ice.

"Unfortunately, when I was just south of the position in which bergs were last reported, the ice report changed and I found to my horror that I was tucked in the angle formed by a line of bergs to the south and a line to the west.

"I was beautifully caught.

"The ice floes come down the eastern side of the Grand Banks in a deep water channel some 60 miles wide, flowing south until they reach the Gulf Stream which turns them east.

"The wind was south-west 5–6 and the fog thick. Even if I tried to turn back and go south-east around the bergs I was liable to find they had moved east since the last sightings, this would lose an awful amount of time anyway and I should find myself back in the unfavourable Gulf Stream.

"The only real course was to cut west straight across the 60 mile ice channel. It was a nerve-racking night beating into the cold fog, waiting for a crash at any moment.

"I packed emergency rations and clothes into a sleeping bag and put this and the emergency life-raft to hand.

"At dawn, when I reckoned myself to be in the middle of the ice channel the wind dropped and the sky cleared. I lay becalmed for most of a beautiful, sunny day, taking my first good sights for a week, and looking at the ice glow on the horizon.

"The *Pilot* says it doesn't show in daylight but I felt sure it was ice glare.

"A U.S. Coastguard cutter found me in the afternoon and I asked where the ice was. They said, 'Where that glow is.' I asked if there was a safe course to miss the ice in the dark, but they reckoned it was a matter of luck.

"At dusk the wind and the fog came back and I had a second night of awful anxiety. At one stage in the middle of the night I was forced by some inner compulsion to heave to for ½ hour, and then I felt much better and was able to sail on. At about 7 knots I kept working out M x V² impact sums and wondered if I should slow down sometimes.

"Dawn was a great relief. I couldn't see any further in the fog, but I had run my distance to be theoretically clear of ice. I only had fishing boats to worry about now."

Both Leslie and Bill were caught at this stage by the Gulf Stream. Bill gave an average for its effect — "a strong current setting us back to the east about 20 miles a day." Leslie was acutely aware of the Stream specifically on the 19th. From a noon sunsight he deduced his longitude as 47°W, adding — "crossing now from Gulf Stream, I think?" Two hours later he noted 46°42′W, and for 1500, after a further sunsight, he wrote 45°50′W, adding — "don't understand error of about 40 miles!!!" This last position plots Leslie about 17 miles ahead of Bill, both of them some 20 miles to the south of the northern ordinary limit of the Gulf Stream.

Earlier that morning Bill had found himself affected by music — "They are playing a stupid, sentimental song about a bloke about to die saying goodbye to his wife and son, on the Homer radio — commercial stuff from St John's! On land I would find myself laughing. But it is funny how the very thought of death touches and oppresses me alone at sea. Perhaps it is because death is closer and so more serious. The thought of losing Gwen, and other people who are close to me (I hate to use the words 'whom I love') really upsets me and brings tears to my eyes and a lump to my throat. Silly perhaps — but that is just how I feel. When I have this hopeless, empty feeling, when I feel so frightened of death, I wish I were back on land, in the rut with the rest of those happy, stupid nuts! I just am never happy, whatever I do, or try to do. Always looking at that other hill over there and wondering what is behind it!"

During the night of the 19th–20th when Leslie hove to for ½ hour from 0030, Bill was tacking to the south to clear the icebergs; diverging from Leslie he sailed himself towards the centre of a calm patch. It affected both boats, but *Golden Cockerel* more severely than *Spirit of Cutty Sark*.

At 0600 Bill wrote that he was becalmed, and then at

1030 — "Very light breeze has sprung up from the north-west and she is doing 3-4 knots in a 5-6 knot breeze, believe it or not. Even in the flattest calm in the great ocean there is always a swell, which rolls the monohull and spills the wind from her sails. This doesn't happen in a multihull, and is certainly one of the reasons that the *Cockerel* slips along in almost no wind.

"1115 Becalmed again.

"1230 A light wind has sprung up from the south-west, but only a ruffle. Sailed for 1 mile, and then becalmed again!

"1330 Have started sailing again.

"1600 Becalmed again.

"1730 Still becalmed in fog and rain!

"2030 Believe it or not, still flat becalmed. This calm set in 16 hours ago. I can only lie in my bunk, putting on the alarm for every hour, waiting for wind.

"Friday 21st June. At 0300 I awoke to the ring of the alarm and saw on the indicator at the foot of my bunk a wind speed outside of 8 knots (becalmed for 21 hours). The wind is building up all the time now."

A calm lasting 21 hours obviously adds all but an extra day to one's crossing time. Bill was however let off lightly indeed compared with Bruce Dalling on a latitude some 70 miles south of him.

The analysis chart for the last chapter shows that Bruce sailed south-west during the 15th and 16th, as did Bill and Leslie, all three boats tacking towards the north around midday on the 17th. For Bruce this turn to the north was made from a position much further south as well as ahead: his midday position on the 17th was as near as makes no odds on the mean centre of the oncoming Gulf Stream.

It had started gripping him by noon on the 15th when his sunsights placed him some 60 miles east of where he had hoped to be; his position at noon on the 16th gave him a similar shock.

On the 14th, as he started this south-west lunge into the Gulf Stream, he had written, "Have decided to rely entirely on the south to south-west winds as forecast in the Pilot charts even though I will be bucking the current."

But as he turned northwards on the 17th the wind started

C*

deserting him. So began what I believe was the most difficult experience anyone had to endure in the race. That evening he started describing it — "I've been sitting in the gloom of the dusk working out with a long face why I can't possibly win now — dogged by misfortune that no one else will have experienced. It never occurs to me that someone else might also be helplessly becalmed. God, what agony I'm going through in this thick head of mine. I've got to get to Sable Island before Saturday to be still in the first half dozen."

18th June — "What a night — the steering gear is all gummed up for some reason–very stiff–and the self-steering can't cope. Had to stay at the helm all night. Tried to free it this morning–checked the self-steering–nothing wrong. Uncoupled it and I could hardly move the thing myself. Got the grease gun out to grease everything, only to find that that is bust as well. So I was left standing there, having achieved absolutely nothing except to get myself covered in black grease. Will have to try and get some sleep as the glass is falling and anything could happen later and will need all my reserves. Hear on the radio that the wind is easterly 15 knots at St John's — just their bloody luck up there. My nerves are starting to jangle again–probably because I'm tired–but it's obvious that I've made a real tactical booboo! The fog isn't very encouraging either. Put my hand into the water to see if I was in the Labrador Current yet–no such luck–fingers came out in one piece. Managed to snatch an hour's sleep — dreamed such horrible dreams I soon woke up in spite of being exhausted . . .

"Am going through mental agony at present — flaying myself for this lack of progress. There is no wind here, and I know everyone else will have a good breeze closer inshore — and the current is killing what little progress I am making . . . When am I going to sleep? Waiting for wind and progress is nearly driving me out of my mind . . .

"A light breeze came through from the west at about 2100 — and just when I was convinced that we were going to be on our way again — it vanished."

19th June — "Took my own advice and slumped in my pit about 0100 and got 6 hours — woke a couple of times but there was still no wind — just shake, rattle and roll

ad nauseam. Dawn brought a sad repetition of yesterday, but
it looks a little more promising as there is some alto-cumulus,
and visibility has improved. Overtook a whale basking on the
surface — about 30–40 yards to port.

"The wind–what there was of it–stayed light all afternoon —
but at least we weren't slatting around — I'm heading north-
west to get out of the Gulf Stream. Sights plotted proved very
disappointing–we're moving but getting nowhere on the
chart–hence the resolve to get into the Labrador Current.
The self-steering is quite incapable of overcoming the friction
now — which means that I have to be at the helm constantly.
Morale is very low, due solely to the fact that I know I must
be doing very badly compared to the others further north.

"Came to the end of the book about Edward Wilson this
afternoon — I nearly cried at the pathos and peace of it all.
What a fantastic example of the Christian life — completely
considered and rational.

20th June — "It's been a helluva night. Didn't manage
to get any sleep at all. Wind veered then died altogether.
The fog and rain came through, and then it came back light
and variable through north. It meant going about, re-adjusting
everything and trying to keep her moving. I can honestly say
that I've worked bloody hard for these miles. I've never seen
weather more changeable than this north Atlantic — the
only steady thing about it is the calms–and possibly the gales–
but there's just nothing in between. No getting everything set
up and sitting back and reading a book etc. in this neck of the
woods. Have been feeling the water regularly — we *still*
aren't out of the Gulf Stream yet. In all my born days I've
never seen weather like this — it's raining buckets now (just
before dawn.) And a God-forsaken dawn it is too–all greys,
no sun, rain and fog–and next to no wind. Morale is rock
bottom through fatigue–physically I am at the very end of my
tether–somehow the mind is just functioning.

"It's all so painfully obvious — morale goes for a burton
when you're tired and the most tiring thing is trying to keep
going when there is no wind. The forecast was for south-west
15 knots — but that's what it's been saying for the last five
days and all that has happened is that we've been becalmed.
This business of having to be at the helm all the time is a

killer. I'm fed up to the back teeth with this frustration.

"I feel so despondent I can hardly write about it. Completely becalmed again and I've just plotted a sight — 107 miles logged and 70 plotted on the chart. We've got a $1\frac{1}{2}$ knot current against us. God — if only I could do something about it. Everything has gone wrong in the last week. It's been four days now. I feel like a man condemned everlastingly — for all the tens of thousands of people at home will never really understand why I did badly. To say you were becalmed for four days when within spitting distance of home sounds awfully pathetic. I can only say that I'm doing my very best — and it's going to take a long time to recover, my whole system is so shot. Decided to occupy myself instead of brooding so checked out the Jap D.F. — still don't know too much about it. Then tidied the chart table, got out new charts etc., tidied the deck and finally, an act of desperado, I climbed the mast to retrieve the topping lift. Got to the top and realised that I hadn't let it go at the bottom, so down I went, undid it, dropped the ghoster and went up a second time and did it properly. Just as I was coming down I heard a fog-horn. I never saw him but he passed close enough to feel the vibration of the note and hear his engines — must have come from the Lakes or Halifax. Morale has improved somewhat and I'm determined I'm still going to get in inside that record. I've got 800 miles to do in a week — it's possible."

Next morning the wind began building up from the south-west. By midday it was blowing a gale, but Bruce was still not clear of his basic trouble — the current; his noon position put him back 40 miles behind his logged distance. However, he wrote — "Morale is far better now" — and then added, "I wouldn't want to go through that one again for all the tea in China."

About 300 miles to the north Brian was sailing *Opus* through the iceberg area. In the early hours of the 21st he saw a "peculiar reflected light in the west like a pink beam, as a rainbow" — and at 0430, "Iceberg sighted where the pink glow was." Brian was cold; as he approached the Virgin Rocks the steering quadrant (part of the vane gear) sheared from the top of the rudder stock — "Had to come below to get feeling in my hands before successfully removing the gear" — 10

hours later the repair was finished. Away from the Gulf
Stream, Brian was making grand progress during this 3 day
period.

There were two further retirements during this stage of the
race. David Pyle sailed *Atlantis III* into Delgada, Santo Miguel
Island, on Wednesday the 19th; his sails were torn, his self-
steering damaged and he was suffering from severe toothache.

Alain Gliksman entered St John's, Newfoundland, on Friday
the 21st. Part of the control for his steering had broken away,
and *Raph* then responded erratically to movements of the
tiller. He gathered a local team on board for the repair work,
but little was done on Saturday. On Sunday no work was done.
On Monday again no work was done — it was the anniversary
of the discovery of the New World; on Tuesday again no
work — it was an election day.

Canadians in general love to tell impossible stories about
Newfoundlanders in particular. The light bulbs in Newfoundland are screwed into their sockets; one is told that it needs
three men to insert a light bulb — one climbs up to hold the
bulb steady and the other two then turn the step ladder round.

Alain left *Raph* up a slip and flew on to Newport.

I have not been able to determine where *Raph* was placed
among the leading yachts in the race. She was sighted by an
aircraft which reported her in a good position on the 6th, but
if there were other favourable sightings they were not passed
to the Royal Western Yacht Club as the official receiver of all
positions for the race.

The analysis chart for this chapter shows the race at an
interesting stage on the 21st — *Cheers* and *Sir Thomas Lipton*
are racing neck and neck, nearly 3 days ahead of a line of
boats formed by *Mex, Spirit of Cutty Sark, Voortrekker* and *Coila*.
The 21 hour calm of *Golden Cockerel* has held her back into the
next rank, more loosely formed with *Opus, Myth of Malham* and
Gancia Girl.

The dramatic feature of this analysis chart is, of course, the
position of *Voortrekker*. Having led in the earlier part of the
race, she has fallen right back in her local calm. The positions
of *Cheers* and *Sir Thomas Lipton* look impregnably far ahead;
behind them, any one of 8 boats could take third place.

During the evening of Friday the 21st Bruce Dalling wrote, "It's as cold as charity" — he was also noting down the details of a tropical cyclone centred 580 miles west-south-west of Bermuda, moving east-north-east at 10 knots with force 11 winds up to 200 miles from the centre.

The leading boats carried receivers capable of picking up weather forecasts direct from shore stations. The news that a hurricane named 'Brenda' was several days distant must have chilled the spine — with weather worse than in the 11th June storm, one could only wait and see in which direction Brenda would move. Anxious eyes were doubtless scanning the diagrams illustrating typical hurricane tracks for June — her possible path would have looked to be anywhere between *Sir Thomas Lipton* to the north and *Rob Roy* to the east. In between was *Cheers*, and Tom Follett wrote at midnight on the 21st–22nd, "Radio reports hurricane brewing south of Bermuda."

Brenda was watched closely at Newport where 152 yachts were waiting to start the Newport–Bermuda race. This major event is organised early in the season, before hurricanes are likely to develop, and not since 1906 had there been more than a 2 hour postponement. Brenda was at first erratic in her behaviour. Bruce correctly noted her expected movement east-north-east, but she then turned north to hover right in the path of the Newport–Bermuda race before moving firmly in an easterly direction. The race was postponed one day to Sunday 23rd June.

During the 23rd Brenda settled on a course that would pass clear to the south of the direct route boats, but their local weather was, nevertheless, awkward during the period 21st–

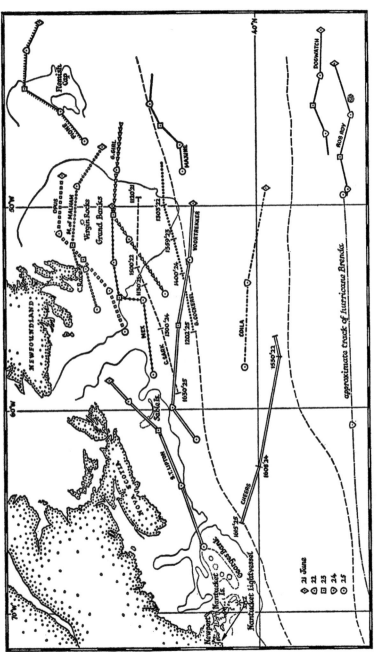

21–25 June

25th: a succession of fronts, inclined to whip up the wind to
gale force, with calm patches in between and cold throughout.
Overnight on the 22nd–23rd Leslie Williams hove to for
3 hours for one front — "A miserable night. Never been so
cold." Bruce had prepared himself for it — "Decided to have
a morale-boosting evening before this gale comes through. Lit
the stove to dry out as much as possible–changed into my last
remaining dry clothes, had a big meal, a few brandies, a cigar,
some good music–and hey presto, here I am patiently waiting
for the – – – – to start flying! Dressed in three pairs of trousers,
vest, shirt, two jerseys, oilskins, balaclava etc. — still cold!"

Tom Follett was edging his way northwards hoping to
give Brenda a wide berth, and this committed him to crossing
the Gulf Stream at this point. He met the difficult conditions
that the Stream can throw up: after a squall of rain the wind
suddenly dies, leaving a short, lumpy sea in which it can be
hard to maintain a course, until another squall abruptly sweeps
overhead.

Further north, *Myth of Malham* had a close shave. At 0145
on the 22nd Noel "was down below. I was very apprehensive
indeed because it was blowing hard–it was fogging hard at
the same time–and I had my ice reports from the International
Ice Patrol which indicated two icebergs on one side for the
same position, and one on the other, and I thought 'well,
I'm all right, I'm more or less in between this lot' — I just
blazed on through the night, going very fast–pounding to
windward–very wet, but really going. The boat suddenly
came up as if the wind had dropped or something had come
adrift. It was a peculiar sensation: from being well heeled and
going fast she shot up, so I went out. At night, under these
conditions, I always have my fluorescent light going on the
backstay, and I saw in the fog, nearly alongside, a sort of mass
which I cannot really describe–it looked yellowish, irregular
and yellowish–but after looking at it for a second or two it was
obviously an iceberg, and all that I can truthfully say is that
I was very frightened and I didn't know what to do. I realised
that it might have a ramp underneath and that it probably
had bergy bits and so on floating in the lee of it. After getting
about ½ mile away from it and thinking hard, I realised that
I hadn't got the nerve to go on and perhaps meet the other

Michael Richey with *Jester*.   *Photo: Eileen Ramsay.*

Sir Thomas Lipton.   *Photo: Chris Smith.*

First arrivals in Newport–Tom Follett, Geoffrey Williams and Bruce Dalling.
Photo: Chris Smith.

one reported in the same position, so I hove to till after dawn."

During this 5 day period Geoffrey Williams had a close shave with the other solid and moving hazard on this leg of the direct route — "After a short sleep I came up on deck and saw eight fishing vessels out astern, some of them Russian. I could not see a clear path through them–they all had trawls out– so God knows how I came through them; I suppose I must have been woken by their sirens." Geoffrey was awkwardly placed between Sable Island and Nova Scotia when he heard the news about Brenda — "I was 'jammed in a box' and in there for 3 days." He worked his boat away from the Nova Scotian coast in difficult winds, as best he could, to give himself more sea room.

The Gulf Stream throws up a short, steep sea particularly when the current is flowing against the direction of the wind. This is awkward for a vessel the size of a yacht, but the Grand Banks can also be dangerous in piling up the waves as they pass over its shoal waters. This is an incident (mercifully not typical!) which happened to Bill Howell early on the 23rd. "At 0300 we were completely overwhelmed by a sudden squall and giant sea which broke clean over the ship and spurted into the cabin through the cracks in the hatchway. The Hepplewhite gear released the sheets and she stopped dead. It was a black bedlam out there — I felt lonely and sick as I struggled to get *Cockerel* back into action fighting the wind and head sea.

"1100 Andrew (McEwen) was delighted that I was having such a tough struggle clearing the Banks — it makes good copy for him for tomorrow's *Mail*.

"1200 The wind has dropped below 20 knots and the barometer is steady — the seas are lining themselves up as long regular swells from the south-west — what a comfortable ride this is after last night's broncobusting!"

The analysis chart shows how Brenda left the Newport–Bermuda race and the direct route well alone, taking instead a straight, fast run towards *Dogwatch* and *Rob Roy*. The U.S. Navy at Washington relayed through two vessels that a southerly course would take *Rob Roy* from the centre of the hurricane — by hindsight I might be forgiven for the feeling in my bones that if a hurricane was coming straight for me there was little I could do to escape!

But this is jumping ahead. To understand the behaviour of *Rob Roy* in the hurricane one should go back to 2025 on the 22nd — at the end of an uneventful day I was trying to raise a ship to report my position. 2182 kc/s, the international voice distress frequency, was suffering from its usual exasperating background clutter of competing voices shouting or pleading to shore stations to answer for routine messages; suddenly a clear and deliberate American voice — "*Holgadanska, Holgadanska*, calling any vessel within range; *Holgadanska*, Whisky X-ray 7575, Whisky X-ray 7575, calling any vessel within range — come in please."

I grinned in appreciation — Americans and Canadians alone show a decisive and endearing character of voice that makes an art of using the radio telephone. But there seemed no point in trying to answer him; like the blind leading the blind, what could one yacht do for another in mid-ocean? I listened again to the impressive voice — on a sudden impulse I picked up my microphone and at once we were speaking to each other. He introduced himself as John Wilson and I replied, "Stephen Pakenham." In this strange encounter we were then uncertain if Christian names or surnames were correct — English formality would have stayed anonymous behind the use of ships' names!

It turned out that he had a powerful set on board and was in touch with a radio ham in Boston, where I subsequently learned that he is a very big name in business circles. He could pass a message with my position, via Boston to England, and we agreed a time to be in touch the next day as he seemed anxious for this. He must have known only too well about Brenda, but would not alarm me with the news as she was shaping her course at that stage hundreds of miles clear to the north.

The next day was certainly eventful — a malaise which had been slowly building up came to a head. I had had an upset stomach since shortly after the start, but the first real sign of trouble came when I was clearing spinnaker lines at the top of the mainmast — suddenly I realised that I was fainting. I came down 40 feet of mast almost as fast as falling, and wobbled along to my bunk. There I slowly recovered, cursing myself for weak nerves; but the next day I nearly lost consciousness again in the exertion of changing two headsails in rapid succession. This time as I recovered on my bunk my thoughts were more constructive — something appeared to be taking a progressive grip on me. Abruptly that grip tightened on the 23rd.

I could not raise any enthusiasm for breakfast. I lay on my back, drained of energy, staring blankly at the reflections of the sun off the waves dancing a golden frenzy across the white deckhead above me. The weather was kind and *Rob Roy* sailed quietly on. A peaceful finality began to creep over me, but when I missed lunch as well as breakfast I realised that I must break this spell quickly or send out a distress call before sundown.

I prayed desperately and with the simplicity of a child — probably the first time in my life that I have asked for help with an unadorned humility. Two ideas came to me, and I tried the easier first: I took a large dose of vitamin C because lethargy is the traditional sign of scurvy. I had, however, been swallowing the tablets intermittently as I remembered them, and so I lay down to wait in vain for any change. Next the fresh water: I had been suspicious of it since the Bay of Biscay because of a peculiar taste and particles floating in it. As I had tried to avoid it, perhaps I was simply suffering from drinking too little. I sat opposite the sink and forced myself to drink a quart slowly — I soon returned it. Gruesome? Revelation will not be put in a straight-jacket by genteel conventions!

I promptly groped my way under the port bunk to a soft plastic container — the water inside looked loathsome with brown blobs in suspension. Despairing, I pulled out the container under the starboard bunk — this water was clear! I cast back in my mind. Where was the container filled? I remembered — $4\frac{1}{2}$ gallons from the bath tap at home would now take me to Newport! I reached for the medicine box for anti-biotics. (At Newport the water was analysed and found to contain a severe contamination of common ecoli: sewage.)

Shortly afterwards I switched on the transmitter when I heard John Wilson's voice. I was trying to think of the right sentence to start explaining that I was nearly incapable of working the boat, but it was clear at once that he had something on his own mind. "Mist-er Packen-ham" he began with careful deliberation–formality obviously the current vogue– "Mist-er Packen-ham — I have some news that I must tell you." I froze against the earphone, my mind flying to an accident at home. Then with great tact he gently broke it to me: he had received a weather report; he carefully gave its time and place of origin; this report concerned a tropical cyclone; it had been tracked for several days; he gave its position and said it was named Brenda, and he quickly added that Brenda was likely to pass to the north. It seemed out of place to mention my own troubles — I quietly agreed to another time for switching on my set to hear how Brenda was moving.

The next day the wind and the sea were slowly building up, and John Wilson said that Brenda had turned eastwards, heading for my position to pass through within the next 24 hours. As he was in touch with the ocean weather vessel, *Echo*, I asked for advice on my best course to steer. John Wilson came back to say that it would have to be referred to Washington; some hours later I was told to steer south. By now I had reduced sail to the working jib only, and I was still going westwards. The course to avoid the heaving heart of Brenda seemed futile—why had I bothered them? If she was coming straight for me on the last report, she might curve north or south before reaching me, and any move on my part would be pointless against her bounding speed. At 1940, however, I did go onto the southerly tack as I suddenly realised I wanted the best chance of a quiet night. I was feeble still, and the antibiotics seemed to be making me giddy. As I began the struggle to winch in the foresheet on the new tack, it was obvious that the wind was blowing on the sail with great force. I took the decision at once to secure *Rob Roy* completely and lie ahull, even though the barograph had hardly yet fallen.

As this race produced so much heavy weather, by way of a different description I quote from a letter to my second son Marcus, then aged 8.

"*Rob Roy* nearing Newport

"Dear Marcus

Your Viking ship picture is beside me as I write this letter: I often look at it and admire it.

As you like the sea I shall tell you about hurricane Brenda. The really lucky thing was that I was in touch with an American yacht, the *Holgadanska*, and she warned me when the hurricane was coming straight for me.

The evening before Brenda was due I slowly and carefully secured everything I could on deck. I screwed pieces of wood over the windows of the doghouse; all of Caroline (self-steering gear) came inside with me; all the sails were carefully furled or stowed below.

Last of all I secured a special piece of wood in front of the companionway, and then I climbed over it, down through the hatch to below where it was warm, snug and dry. I had a jolly good supper, and then a funny thing happened. You see, I had been sailing *Rob Roy* for 23 days without stopping, so as she was lying so comfortably, heeling nicely to the wind and quite steady, I went absolutely fast asleep!

Occasionally I half-woke when a wave broke over *Rob Roy*, but she did not mind that, so I did not get up to ask how she was; she was obviously doing fine.

I am glad to say that I woke up in time for breakfast in the morning, and when I popped my head out of the hatch I was surprised by a strangely beautiful sight: the eye of the hurricane had arrived right over me. I knew this because the sun was shining and the wind was all over the place, quite soft, with the sea very confused. At least 'confused' is the description generally used. I would have described it as looking thoroughly astonished. Everywhere there were tiny little waves plopping straight up and down as though a million fish were trying to jump into the air, but could not quite make it. The big swell tried to move along pompously in one direction, but when it started to break a crest down its front the wind blew it back as spray in the opposite direction.

I finished a pot of honey with my breakfast, and I screwed the top back on and dropped it overboard. I'm sure that

Pooh would have agreed that this was entirely the appropriate thing to do in the eye of a hurricane.

The honey jar bobbed up and down beside me until I yawned in the warm sunshine and went below again to sleep.

When I woke up the sun had disappeared behind low cloud scudding over a tumbling sea. The barograph was shooting up as steeply as it had tumbled down, so I knew that the eye of Brenda was moving away as fast as it had come.

I hope that a mermaid found the jar of honey and put a note inside reading 'I was launched in the eye of a hurricane.'

Love
Daddy"

Rob Roy came through the hurricane entirely unscathed apart from two minor matters: a neat slit, just an inch long, appeared in the furled mizzen — I found no way of explaining it; also, I lashed the helm securely but with only one length of cordage — it chafed through, and a good deal of wood was rubbed away.

The experience of Brenda was simpler and more brutal for Nigel Burgess — he received no warning of her approach. On the 20th, to help his fast passage, he poured 15 gallons of fresh water over the side–half his supply–remarking, "It is a beautiful day — I think really the best we have had so far. I do hope this weather lasts." The next day, "The weather is still fabulous." On the 23rd 4 gallons of paraffin went over the side with the wooden parts of his toilet. He was unscrewing inesssential joinery in the cabin, and even chucked out Pilot books and charts "when I discovered I was not going near Canada — everything which would lighten the boat went over the side."

Early on the 24th he was almost becalmed — and then it began: "I got out of my bunk at 0600 on Monday morning and it just started to blow; it got worse steadily during the day until about 1600 it was force 8 gusting 9. The self-steering gear was smashed off the boat by a sea at 1900 — an eyebolt fractured on the transom, and the gear was knocked sideways and smashed off. It blew all through that night. I still had sail up when it was force 8, and I kept the sail up until midday the next day. Then it started to get very close and the sky cleared and there was a most fantastic calm. Usually when we get a big wind shift there is a calm when you lie there and the sails slat, and of course if it has been force 8 the seas are very high. You have got very high waves and then suddenly it all goes dead and everything just slops around. It is rather like being in a swimming pool when all the people have got out of it — really quite horrible! When you are alone and all the people have got out there is this sort of lop and you bounce around like a cork, very unpleasant.

"Well, I suspected something was up — you do when you get this. The sky had cleared — the sun shone. I put up the full mainsail; I put up the largest genoa jib as I had a storm jib on for the previous day, through that night and into Tuesday morning. Anyway, I got the whole lot up again. I waited one hour before I put all these sails up, thinking if nothing happened in the hour all would be okay. Nothing did happen — the wind stayed flat calm. Then at 1230 a great long black line squall appeared on the horizon to the north — a great big black line squall. First of all there was this lovely sun, and then the wind started as a slight breeze from the north, and then I could see it. With these very high waves it is like going up and down in a lift. You go up to the top right onto to the crest and you can see for miles around and it is great. When you are in the trough you can't see a thing. I could see this wind slowly coming towards us. I didn't have time to react, but anyway it must have been travelling at 30 or 40 miles-an-hour and already in 5 minutes I was in the first squall which must have been about force 8 or 9, and then it was up to 10 plus. I whipped the mainsail off as fast as I could–everything off–everything down below, and in 15 minutes I was was under bare poles running before it (streaming ropes, etc.). The previous day's wind had come from the south and south-west and it went through to north or slightly north-north-east — the exact reciprocal to the seas."

It calmed down during the evening, and the next morning Nigel re-rigged the self-steering gear using a deck eyebolt to replace the broken one.

Why did we come through Brenda with comparative ease? Three reasons can be given. The first — her course was straight; if a hurricane turns in a circle, the confusion of wave directions can be lethal for a yacht if the sea topples over as the waves rear up against each other. The second — her centre was travelling fast; a strong wind needs time to build up its potential height of wave. The third and most important reason — Brenda's wind was apparently barely at hurricane strength; a wind of 245 knots was recorded in America in 1958, nearly 4 times the 64 knot minimum for a hurricane. Had Brenda circled, slowed down, or blown harder, our experience would surely have been altogether different, or never written at all!

On Sunday the 23rd came news of another retirement — *La Delirante*, sailed by L. Paillard, was sighted returning to France. I am told that her mast was broken — unfortunately I have no other details.

The analysis chart for this chapter shows *Voortrekker* overhauling *Cheers* and *Sir Thomas Lipton*, but it looks too late for her to pass them. Her chart position at midday on the 25th is 374 miles from the Nantucket Lightvessel — about a 24 hour run behind them and a big gap as *Cheers* is shown 2 days or so from the finish.

Cheers was probably narrowly in the lead, allowing for *Sir Thomas Lipton's* 12 hour penalty and the fact that *Cheers* had just left the Gulf Stream area for a clear run to the lightvessel, whereas *Sir Thomas Lipton* had the length of St George's Bank to negotiate. *Cheers* is shown 175 miles from the lightvessel at 1615 on the 25th.

12 Three in, four out *25-28 June*

I am very grateful to Geoffrey Williams for a tape recording which he gave me shortly after the finish, explaining the final run in of *Sir Thomas Lipton.*

During the night of the 25th–26th *Sir Thomas Lipton* "went right over the George's Bank." This was perhaps the first sign of a desperate finish; carrying his penalty, Geoffrey had to keep a half day's run ahead — the chart marks the shallowest patch on St George's Bank as 9 feet and *Sir Thomas Lipton* has a draft of 8 feet.

"I was spotted as 60 miles ahead of *Voortrekker*, and to the north of him . . . This made it important as I had read the sailing instructions and was very surprised to see — 'Oh! I go south of Nantucket, not south of Nantucket Lightvessel as I had always told the computer people and told everyone else. This is strange — what do I do?' Well, I have done enough yacht racing to know and always be advised by the written instructions. I was expecting to go south at Nantucket Light-vessel. Then I looked at the chart and saw that they had moved the lightvessel about 6 miles further south. It was certainly since the previous race; in fact it was only on my chart correction which was done 10 days before the race. So I thought this might have entered their reasoning, pushing it further south and leaving a very sizeable gap between the northern limit of the very dense shipping lane and the southern limit of the shoal area on Nantucket Shoals. 'Oh!' I thought, 'the Committee is being really sensible in letting us choose our own way between the shipping lane and the shoals.'

"I was going along quite happily, force 5 on the beam from the south, and suddenly–with no warning–this has never happened to me before (I had the mizzen staysail up —

luckily I had a preventer on the boom) the wind came from a different direction — instead of from the south it came from the north-north-east, and it swung before the self-steering gear had any time to compensate. I was faced with a tear in my mizzen staysail. Luckily the preventer held — it did not tear the mizzen staysail, although the boom did touch the sail. I got the mizzen staysail down. Then the wind got right up, very strong indeed; I had my light weather ghoster up but because my foresail and mainsail were to some extent shielding it with this wind behind me I decided to keep it up — just bring the mizzen staysail down. After about an hour I had a force 8 wind on the clock.

"When I was north of the lightvessel I called . . . I had forgotten my tide tables, and I asked them to give me tide times for Pollock Rip; so I knew what was very important to know if the wind went light, which way I was going to be whisked–onto the shoals or away–and I had about 4 hours to get through the shoals with a south moving tide.

"I shaved — I didn't go less than 4 fathoms because the sea was very confused, very broken, and in fact there were acres of breaking water north and south of my course. I had chosen my course between the rips, between the 4 fathom marks . . . absolutely determined to keep ahead of *Voortrekker*, and by going high on the shoals I knew I would be forcing him outside me all the time, because I knew he did not have Loran."

Those who were waiting at Newport were alerted to the position of *Sir Thomas Lipton* by the call which Geoffrey made. Colonel Odling-Smee, Chairman of the Race Committee, was placed on the horns of a dilemma. Geoffrey's course through the shoals was his own responsibility, but if Colonel Odling-Smee ordered him to wear to the south to round the Nantucket Lightvessel, and if the new course proved lethal . . . Colonel Odling-Smee thought hard and fast while Geoffrey waited for his decision — then he told him to follow his sailing instructions as printed, and Geoffrey sailed on through shoals "that no yacht on this coast could dare to go into" — as he was later told.

Once through the shoals he turned northwards for the final 76 miles leg to Newport. "Buzzards Light was the first one I saw." He was now about 2 hours from the finish.

"It was very difficult to pick up the finish with all the land lights behind, and the Brenton Reef Tower did not start flashing away until much later than I had expected, so I was quite befuddled for a while until I saw a green flashing light behind it which was on the chart, and this verified the position.

"That was the finish; totally happy–rather tearfully, I remember–and completely satisfied. All this nonsense about penalties and going the wrong side of the light seemed rather frivolous and irrelevant. I had done what I wanted to do, and set out to do seven years ago, and I was completely satisfied."

Various estimates have been given for the time that Geoffrey Williams saved by sailing north of the Nantucket Lightvessel. The question is whether he saved more than 5 hours 9 minutes (5 hours 9 minutes + 12 hours of penalty = 17 hours 9 minutes, the time by which he came in first.) In my opinion he would have needed more than 5 hours 9 minutes to cover the dog leg south for rounding the lightvessel, *if* he had left this until on or near the shoals.

At the briefing session the Race Committee had made it clear that competitors were to pass south of the lightvessel, but Geoffrey Williams left at one point to answer a telephone call.

Geoffrey arrived at 0233 on Thursday 27th June. I am told that a number of the boats which put out into the dark to meet him were expecting to welcome *Cheers* — what had happened to her?

At 0950 on the 26th, while Geoffrey was rapidly closing the Nantucket Shoals, Tom Follett was writing, "Fluky wind. All sails off till it settles down. Looks like I'm trapped here 135 miles from the Nantucket light."

It seems that *Sir Thomas Lipton* and *Cheers*, less than 80 miles apart, were not sharing the same weather. As Geoffrey turned northwards after crossing the shoals, Tom wrote, "Very lumpy seas tossing us about. Still, we make a little progress on course to the lightship. What dreary weather! Worse than England. Never have seen such fluky winds as we are having today." Geoffrey was well-placed to be north, clear of it.

Bruce Dalling, in the same weather as Tom, was overhauling him with tremendous determination. During the forenoon of the 26th he set a spinnaker having heard a gale forecast abaft his beam. He kept his spinnaker flying–the wind occasionally gusting force 7–and during the night he passed Tom. At 0840 the next morning he rounded the lightvessel and turned northwards for Newport. It was now a shy reach for the spinnaker — "It kept dipping in the water and she gave every indication of being too hard pressed, so I handed the kite and used all plain sail, covering the distance between the lightvessel and the finishing line at an average of 10.1 knots."

The approach of *Cheers* and *Voortrekker* to the lightvessel is one of the fascinating episodes of the race; I have made a parallel analysis from their logbooks which is in an appendix. There is also a rough diagram opposite, made possible because the log readings of both boats were recorded at the lightvessel. I have drawn two straight lines backwards from those readings; it is not an exact comparison–both boats are drawn as if sailing straight–but it does give an idea of the manner in which *Voortrekker* passed *Cheers*.

Tom passed 25 yards from the lightvessel at 1120 and for 7 hours chased Bruce. At 1830 however he lowered all sail for 2 hours — "Running down under bare poles. Too much wind for control." At 1942 Bruce crossed the finishing line. At 2030 Tom set his foresail again until 2315 when once more he was down to bare poles — "Heavy rain. Shocking weather. Drifting along on course." $1\frac{1}{2}$ hours later he was about to be blown over the finishing line, so he "hoisted the foresail off Brenton Reef to jill about until daylight. Stormy night and I'd rather wait." He waited $4\frac{1}{4}$ hours until daylight, and crossed the line to finish third at 0620 on the 28th.

Cheers was clearly at a disadvantage during the final run in, but the measure of Tom's achievement in the race lies in the 40 foot length of *Cheers* compared with the 50 feet of *Voortrekker* and 56 feet of *Sir Thomas Lipton* — by any conceivable system of handicap between the three, *Cheers* would have been first on corrected time.

The diagram giving the finish on a time scale shows how the first three boats arrived relatively close to each other. Count Bertrand de Castelbajac wrote a book shortly after the race which he dedicated to Bruce Dalling *qui préféra être second avec élégance que premier sans panache*. This refers, of course, to the possibility of an appeal, but Bruce Dalling firmly rejected

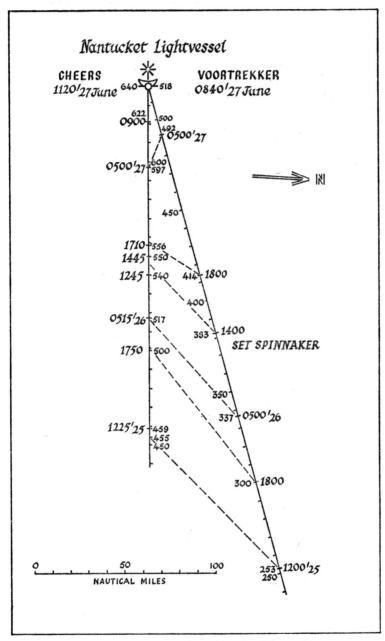

Cheers and *Voortrekker* approaching Nantucket lightvessel.

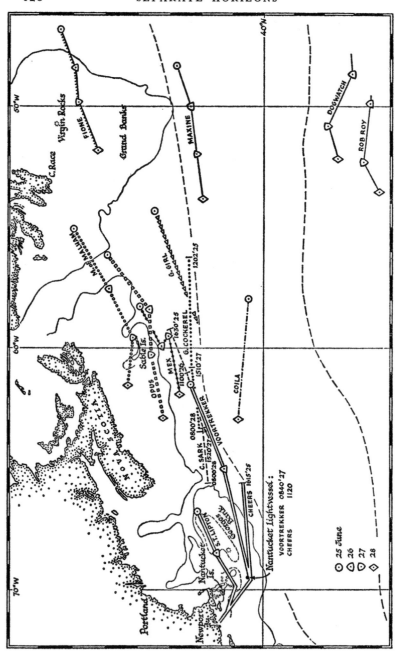

25–28 June

any suggestion of making a protest.

At this period of the race four boats were leaving it.

Edith Baumann was the only woman competitor in the race; aged 26, her home is in Aachen, Germany. Her boat *Koala III* was designed and built by Commandant Waquet who also gave her an intense 6 month course in seamanship and navigation during the year before the race. Her 39 foot trimaran sloop was fitted with an anti-whale bar and hydro brakes to stop it running away down wind.

She was following the Azores route until the morning of the 26th when her S.O.S. was picked up by the Italian liner *Michelangelo*, and relayed to Lloyds.

The full scale air and sea search was overshadowed by the approaching hurricane Brenda. American and French aircraft and four French warships were searching north of the Azores.

Reports were received that she had abandoned her trimaran as breaking up, and had taken to her black life-raft. This proved to be false when a U.S. Air Force plane found the boat with Edith Baumann still on board, 320 miles north-north-east of Graciosa. With her dog, Shatz, her constant companion, she was picked up by the French warship *Henri Poincaré* to be landed in Brest.

The Italian Alex Carozzo entered Falmouth on Thursday the 27th. *San Giorgio*, his powerful 53 foot catamaran, had been described as a possible winner in the race. It would be interesting to know how well he had been racing, but I know no more than that he had a failure in his steering gear to cause his retirement.

Rob Roy sustained crucial damage, also on the 27th. At 1500 I entered a west-north-west wind in the log, and at 1848, in a distinctly shaky hand — "Hove to starboard tack." Having been hove to for two nights and one day in hurricane Brenda, I was over-anxious to catch up — I may have underestimated the rising head wind into which I was forcing *Rob Roy*. At 1730 Nigel Burgess had already hove to — "I just could not stand the pounding. It is blowing 7–8, gusting 9, possibly more at times. I can't see the point in smashing myself up unnecessarily." A Canadian escort minesweeper not far to the west recorded a gust of 75 knots (well into the hurricane range.) I hove to when the stem scarfing worked loose — water was spurting in on every bounce of the bows. Once hove to, the stem looked happy, and it was several days before I realised that for *Rob Roy* the race–as a race–was over.

For Eric Willis on board *Coila* events took place with dramatic speed. "After I had been lying to very heavy weather (the northern edge of hurricane Brenda) I picked up a radio message from Radio Halifax that the weather was easing. I made a note in the log–'sails up soon, in the meantime a meal'–the next thing I became aware of after this was that two men were climbing over the rail — they seemed almost like mermaids. In fact, two paramedics had arrived on board, having dropped from an aircraft in thick fog.

"Apparently the main cause of the trouble was due to the failure of a hose clip on the outlet from the heads. This had cracked and allowed a leak which, in the very hot weather, produced a clear transparent slime, and in the course of pulling up the log to clear the weed this had contaminated my hands and must have got transferred to food.

"The illness itself resulted in almost complete blindness, lack of hearing, loss of use of my legs and to some extent apparently, sickness, the side effects being tremendous temperature and ultimately complete dehydration.

"Apparently I radioed Halifax for medical advice (on Sunday the 30th) and petered out on them having been told to go onto stand-by. Getting no answer from me, Halifax Radio put the message through to Pease Air Base near Portland, Maine, where they decided that something had to be done quickly. They took approximately 4 minutes to make the decision to alert full services, call out the Coast Guard vessel, *Acushnet*, and organise themselves to be over my position at dawn—which they did. They dropped smoke flares at the position quoted, did a run and came back, having put the figures through a computer at Pease Air Base; they picked me up on the radar 7 miles away where they saw the orange deck through the fog. They jumped immediately on the first run.

"The paramedics were two of the nicest possible boys you could meet, and if you met them in the street you would never think they had done anything. When I asked them why they were fool enough to jump into the Atlantic they said they

were bored with Service subjects and were glad of something
different to do — it was all good training!

"They had apparently spent 10 years training for this job:
to go down for astronauts. Before taking it up they were
survival instructors with the U.S. Air Force. The training itself
required the ability to fly an aeroplane, ride a horse, sail a
boat, do deep diving, operate a glider or cut one's liver out
if in the mood. They were, in fact, fully qualified surgeons and
carried their own drugs with them as well.

"The photograph obtained from Pease Air Base was taken
from the aircraft immediately after the drop — Sergeant
Treudle is on deck and Staff Sergeant Litchnovsky is still in the
water."

The paramedics were dropped from a turbo-prop transport
of the 54th Aerospace Rescue and Recon Squadron's para-
rescue section. When the *Acushnet* arrived, Eric was taken on
board and *Coila* towed back to Portland, Maine—under
medical care, Eric soon recovered.

13 A pause for two
28 June - 2 July

While still at sea, Bruce Dalling wrote — "I think a lot about those in the small boats who will be 6 or 7 weeks at sea–(I always imagine myself in the Vertue)–I think it is them that are the really tough ones, not ourselves in the bigger, faster, more comfortable boats. Bigger boats require more physical strength and far more method, but the little ones require more stamina and seamanship."

For those casually interested, it might have seemed that the race was now over — the first three boats had arrived in quick succession, and there followed an interval of 58 hours before the next one came in.

For those still sailing, it was far from over! Apart from the aim to arrive by 31st July to qualify as a finisher, there was the monohull handicap: *Opus* was approaching fast enough to win, and *Fione* was well placed to take advantage of any last minute trouble to Brian Cooke.

Trouble came to Brian in no small measure on the 29th when a near gale force wind collapsed everything in front of his mast. "It happened about 9 o'clock in the morning. I was down below changing my clothes from wet to dry — there was a sudden bang which was the bits of the halyard winch landing on the deck; it had sheared away from its fitting on the mast. That was bad enough in itself, but almost immediately I noticed that the genoa and the forestay were all tangled up, half over the side and half on board as a result of this halyard winch shearing; I concluded that the strain or jerk at the mast-head had been the cause of the tang breaking — both happened simultaneously.

"The mast was bending back like a carrot, bending, I should think, at least 20°, if not more, from the hounds. I didn't think

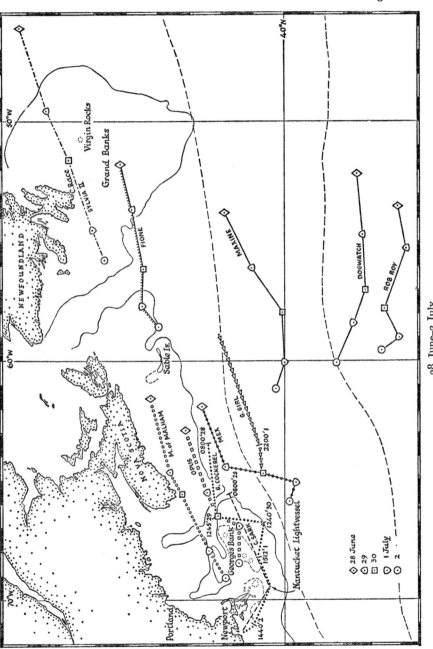

28 June–2 July

there was a hope of saving the mast, but I immediately took the mainsail off to take the way off the boat as the genoa was being towed in the water. I got the genoa and the tangle of forestay aboard, and the spinnaker halyard was rigged in pretty quick order as a jury forestay.

"The boat was rolling a lot with no sail to steady her, and I got pretty wet — as I say, I was changing at the time and had to carry out the operation in my underwear. I was worried about putting too much strain on the jury forestay fitting until I had been able to do something more permanent, but that was out of the question at the time — I think it would have been suicidal to try and go up the mast in those conditions.

"I put up the mainsail reefed first of all, reefed because I thought a full mainsail would be too much strain on the top of the mast, and on its own the mainsail just kept the boat steady with no appreciable forward motion.

"I set two small foresails flying — very ineffective going to windward because, having no halyard winches, I had to set them up with handy-billies, and the deck was like a cat's cradle with lines and tackles going everywhere. I could not head closer than about 6 points to the wind. With the leeway we were making we were getting into shallower water and shorter seas — it was a case of sailing 100 miles through the water to make good about 48.

"The wind died down quite a bit after 36 hours — I put the big genoa up which was much more productive. On the third day this had given me 48 hours to plan how I was going up the mast when conditions were suitable."

Brian's entry in his logbook then gives a detailed account for Monday 1st July:

"0800 One Russian trawler passed 50 yards off–we were both blasting our fog signals–several others in the vicinity. Visibility about 50 yards as trawler was only just visible.

"Quite a swell, but it is as calm as it will be; must have a go at the masthead fitting, so:—

1. Got all tools with spares of each ready in a bucket.
2. One pin (only spare) and four split pins (in case I dropped some.)
3. Got stays lashed to ladder so that I could handle them aloft (they are very heavy with 46 feet of wire and

bottle-screws on them.)

4. Bucket with tools lashed to ladder.
5. Hoisted ladder to masthead.
6. Took half a dozen short lengths of line on my shoulder for stopping off ladder as I went up.
7. Said a prayer that I might be given strength to do the job.
8. Lowered mainsail — put yacht on course with wind abeam to minimise movement aloft.

"Did job aloft (hit on the head with swinging forestay fitting — thought I was going to black out.)

"Came down, unscrambling gear.

"Said a prayer of thanks.

"Set up rigging screws, up mainsail and big genoa hanked on — all set and so marvellous to feel the yacht alive again and moving through the water with a nice wake and sails sheeted in properly.

"Am greatly bruised, chafed and scratched doing the job, but oh! the elation has made me not worry a bit about the discomfort."

It is not easy trying to estimate the time lost by Brian–probably between 1 and 2 days–but it brought *Myth of Malham* abreast and, more important, it allowed *Fione* to catch up on handicap.

After 4 days of gales–Brenda in the middle–Nigel Burgess wrote on the 28th, "A beautiful day, how about that" — the next day he set his spinnaker to complete his best day's run of 124 miles. He was, despite Brenda, holding a good position against *Maxine* to the north.

To the south, *Rob Roy* was faltering. I would not have described the leak in the bow as dangerous yet — the question was how it might deteriorate. A contrast in sailing conditions was astonishing me: when the wind was free–the bow rising and falling smoothly over the waves with no jerking of the forestay–I could sail as though nothing had happened; against a head wind above force 3, I could do nothing except heave to or change direction as, if the bow started butting, the leak manifestly increased. With this in mind, I was thinking ahead to choppy seas in the Gulf Stream, and Bermuda to the south-west looked on the chart like a stepping stone. I would

take several days closing it and have time to assess the leak.
If I then sailed on it would be only a few more days to Newport
and, above all, the prevailing winds would be astern and
the Gulf Stream crossed at a better slant.

If I could no longer race, it seemed obvious to try and be
seamanlike. The decision came swiftly on the 2nd — the
midday position showed that I had stopped racing in otherwise
good winds, and within 5 minutes I had tacked to the south.

The analysis chart for this chapter shows *Sylvia II* appearing
from behind like a shooting star. André Foëzon had been
dismasted the 3rd day out from Plymouth. 5 days were then
needed to sail back, and a further 3 days for the mast repair.
Undaunted, he sailed out of Plymouth Sound on 12th June,
determined to achieve the fastest time on handicap. He did
not sight Cape Race, but passed close by on the 30th "frightened
for my skin" in a force 11 wind.

5 hours after his dismasting, *Mex* had passed him 100 metres
away — "*personne sur le pont!*" *Mex*, from challenging the lead
on the 18th, had now slipped to 8th position in the race.

Spirit of Cutty Sark took 4th place, crossing the finishing line
at 1617 on the 30th. *Golden Cockerel* came in 5th at 2224 on
2nd July.

The two of them had been a day apart at 0800 on the 28th;
they then made an approach to the Nantucket Lightvessel
which compares with that by *Voortrekker* and *Cheers*, in each
case the monohull gaining more than a day.

The picture of what was happening becomes a little clearer
with *Spirit of Cutty Sark* and *Golden Cockerel*. Early on the 28th
Leslie Williams wrote, "Here we go again. Wind dead aft —
making weaving course at 8 knots with abominable gyrations.
There seems no answer to it. It is driving me mad. Those
multihulls must be screaming up behind, chuckling" —
this he wrote when the wind was force 5; as it increased, his
course steadied and the boat moved faster.

For Bill Howell it happened the other way round: as the
wind increased, he began to lose control — "Having a really
heavy ride . . . touching 15 knots in bursts, going rather
dangerously in wind gusts. Too much for my nerves, especially
as the wind vane will not work when she hits the high speeds

and yaws downwind. There is just not enough apparent wind then to turn the vane to bring her back on course.

"I dropped the No. 2 topsail and mizzen and am sailing sedately along at 8 knots, except occasionally when she hits over 10 knots as she takes off downwind. She is broad reaching, and she just accelerates too fast — these cats need two men, at least, as they have to be watched for these sudden bursts of speed . . . up to 8 knots on all points of sailing, the wind vane self-steering is happy. Beyond 8 knots it begins to complain, and by 12 knots it is in trouble."

The next day Bill wrote, "Wind gusting up to gale force. I have dropped all sail and am slanting across this south-east blow at 5 knots under bare poles. Progress too slow, so raised storm jib, and am now doing 7 knots." He crossed the finishing line 2 days 6 hours 7 minutes after Leslie.

Brian Cooke rounded the Nantucket Lightvessel at 1900 on 3rd July, leaving it just 10 yards to starboard — "12 bodies lined the deck to gawp; they said they had seen no yachts today."

Brian was then becalmed between the lightvessel and the finishing line. At midday on the 4th — "The most frustrating day of the trip. It is an absolute mill-pond; as soon as I leave the helm she goes aback . . . the only land seen in this ride so far is Sable Island in the distance." At 1800 — "Has been calm for 3 hours solid and we are not moving; 36 miles to go." The next day brought thick fog. With radio beacons and a fog signal he navigated himself over the middle of the finishing line at 1423 without seeing the marks at either end — then he sighted America!

Less than 5 hours later Martin Minter-Kemp brought in *Gancia Girl* as the first trimaran home, the 7th boat to finish in the race. While Martin was stowing his sails to be taken in tow, Noel Bevan was becalmed in thick mist in the shipping lane which runs straight from the Nantucket Lightvessel to the Ambrose Lightvessel outside New York. Noel had been dogged by calms for several days — the last 35 miles to the Nantucket Lightvessel had taken some 21 hours. His fortune changed at 1530 the next day and he crossed the finishing line at 0741 on the 7th.

Of those now left at sea, *Maxine* and *Dogwatch* are shown nearest the Nantucket turn. *Rob Roy* had been diverging from Newport for 2 days on the best tack to close Bermuda, but then an exhilerating force 3 wind from the south gave two 24 hour runs of 130 and 150 miles; with little working of the bow in the beam wind, Bermuda was quickly forgotten as a possible

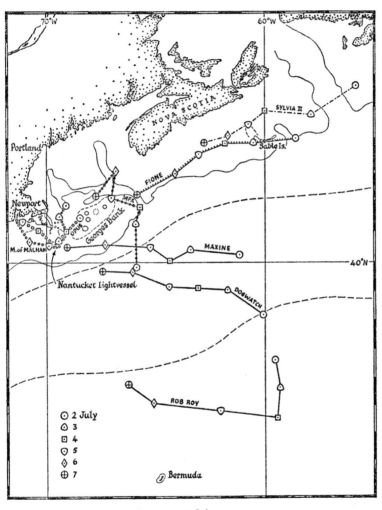

2-7 July

refuge! On the 7th she entered Gulf Stream weather for several days of "calms and light airs relieved only by fierce winds revolving round tightly-formed thunderstorms."

Fione and *Sylvia II* sailed into the area between Sable Island and Nova Scotia — that stretch of water seems almost like glue! Both boats show sluggish progress on the analysis chart; *Sylvia II*, nearer inshore, was affected more than *Fione*.

15 A bunch of seven   *7 - 13 July*

As Bertrand de Castelbajac passed the Nantucket Lightvessel on the 7th, the crew said that 6 yachts in the race had passed by. Bertrand was another who approached the finish in fog; he crossed the line at 1947 on the 8th — the first Frenchman home.

The next boat was also French — Jean Yves Terlain sailed *Maguelonne* 10th across the line at 1510 on the 9th. I have not obtained a track for *Maguelonne*, but a northern route was planned, the line across the chart passing closely north of the Virgin Rocks and 10 miles south of Sable Island. She was apparently well south of this route when at 1318 on the 27th she was sighted by a Canadian aircraft which gave a position inside the Gulf Stream area.

Nigel Burgess followed Jean Yves Terlain by 3 hours 3 minutes. Because of the small size of *Dogwatch*, Nigel jumped 3 places on handicap, beating *Maxine* on corrected time by the bare margin of 2 hours 16 minutes. So ended the intriguing contest between *Maxine*, *Dogwatch* and *Rob Roy* (*Rob Roy* was wallowing in thunderous calm several days distant!)

Next in at 0616 on the 11th was André Foëzon in *Sylvia II*. His official placing is, of course, as he finished, 12th by time elapsed from the starting gun on 1st June; but the Race Committee certified his actual passage time as 29 days 16 minutes which gives a corrected time of 21 days 10 hours 27 minutes, and that is a record passage on handicap by 1 day 6 hours 24 minutes. Other boats gave up after being dismasted; the determination and ability of André Foëzon has surely established him on a level with Eric Tabarly, Bruce Dalling and Tom Follett.

Later that evening *Fione* crossed the line unnoticed at 2013

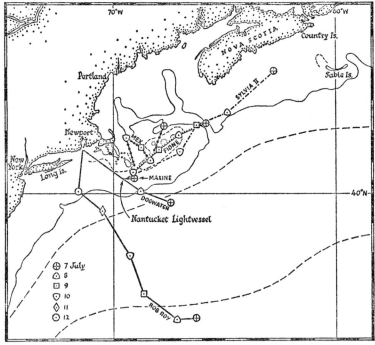

7–13 July

and motored up harbour to find a berth for the night. The next day her time was established as second on handicap; Brian Cooke had to drop to 3rd place for the extra 1 hour 52 minutes in his corrected time, but Bruce Dalling remained the handicap winner.

Bertil's elapsed time of 40 days 14 hours 13 minutes highlights the strides which this race has made — *Gipsy Moth III* won the first race in 40 days 12 hours 30 minutes. That race finished at New York, a further day's run down the coast, but *Gipsy Moth III* is 39 feet 7 inches long compared with *Fione's* 19 feet 8 inches!

What were the factors behind Bertil's success? He was always meticulous in choosing the best tack for following the direct route, never tiring of putting the boat about on a shift of wind, and never sleeping for more than ½ hour at a time. On the other hand, he avoided the temptation to 'pinch', sailing as much as 10° free from the close-hauled course so that *Fione's* hull would keep moving at good speed. He must have been energetic and effective in his sail changes — he set one of his two spinnakers about 10 times; but above all, Bertil has a very methodical mind which leaves nothing to chance: his preparations for the race were extremely thorough.

Mex crossed the line at 1646 on the 12th. Her final 17 days at sea may seem to present an enigma — Claus Hehner said he had persistent calms.

Finally in this bunch of seven, *Rob Roy* was carried over the line by the tide at 0949 on the 13th, all sail set and filled with little more than a balmy sun. The erratic track for the last 16 days shows to some extent how she was hove to in every sea that worked the bows. I felt at the time that I never wished to race again — it seemed poor seamanship to have driven a beautiful boat so ruthlessly. I had of course over-driven her and then paid for it accordingly.

It may seem strange that earlier I described *Rob Roy* as "leaving the race," but her finish was truly fortunate: she was the one boat substantially damaged in the hull which made Newport rather than another harbour on the way. I had asked for the race number 'seven' for its biblical symbolism of plenty. Most people connect seven with good luck; in fact I had plenty of wind and incident *and* good luck!

16 Glory is the shadow of virtue

13 - 28 July

Colin Forbes sailed in at 1608 on the 16th to find a heat-wave shimmering the shore. As with *Maguelonne*, unfortunately I have no track for *Startled Faun*. Colin returned quickly to England to start condensing some 4½ hours of footage shot for a ½ hour film for Watney Mann.

Bernard Rodriquez arrived in *Amistad*, another trimaran, at 0005 on the 19th — "I thought I was going to have fun; I sailed right in in the fog–cooking the stew–and I almost hit the rocks!" He found a cove near the finishing line for an anchorage until morning.

In 1967 Bernard was first on handicap in a New York to Bermuda race for multihulls, but he had had two set backs before the start of this race: a very rough and slow Atlantic crossing to Plymouth left little time to recover before racing back; worse still, in Plymouth he heard that Arthur Piver had been lost at sea while on his qualifying cruise for the race. Piver was a famous pioneer American designer of trimarans, *Startled Faun* and *Amistad* being two examples of his work. Bernard had expected to find Arthur Piver smiling and waiting for him in Plymouth — the news of his loss must have been a great shock.

Bernard had selected a great circle route, but again I have no track; he was edging his way southwards on his route when he realised that he was running out of food — he had been shopping in Plymouth with Joan de Kat, whose witty and unending flow of conversation may just possibly have distracted him from buying sufficient stores — or at least that is the popular story! Bernard then sailed north onto the Grand Banks where he "spent a good deal of time lying ahull to strong winds, or sitting becalmed." Eventually he was able to approach the Nova Scotian coast and selected the Country Island radio beacon for homing himself in. Behind the island he found Seal Harbour where he stayed 10 hours replenishing his stores.

The next man in was another who had been shopping with Joan de Kat. Åke Mattsson is a Swede, a mechanical engineer by profession, and manager of a department of technical information writing. He had bought two 4-gallon water containers in Plymouth, not noticing the weakness of their seals. They were laid in the forepeak to be left to the last, and by the time Åke came to them they had shaken out all but a little of their fresh water. He made the discovery 200 miles south of Cape Race. As he planned to turn northwards to sail down wind for Newfoundland, he found himself headed; he turned back towards Sable Island and the wind fell light. His thirst increased as he soaked his dried food in salt water to make it edible. He contacted Radio Halifax when his situation became desperate, and the next morning a Canadian aircraft found him at first light to drop a water cylinder 100 yards away.

It seems very rough luck that Åke had to be disqualified for receiving outside assistance, but the Race Committee obviously had no choice. He sailed into Newport at 0148 on the 22nd.

This story of the 1968 race ends with the arrival of Michael Richey in *Jester*. He had sailed "off the map" on 15th June, ploughing his lonely furrow southwards for the Trade Wind route where, incidentally, he became 51 on 6th July, the birthday "celebrated by a squall only!"

"The north-east Trade Wind finally came in at about $27\frac{1}{2}°$N on 20th June, after numerous hesitant easterly breezes, and except for a lull on the 29th, in about 45°W, it took me across the ocean, making daily runs of the order of 140 miles in the most pleasant conditions, with fresh quartering winds, a brilliant blue sea and hot sun. I had by now settled down to an ordered existence. Within the framework of the daily tasks–navigating and sailing the boat, cooking, eating and sleeping–one has somehow to achieve a way of life which satisfies, not by means of distractions but rather by coming to terms with the situation. Being able to live positively under these rather improbable conditions and to enjoy the world is more than half the point. It seems important, for example, to eat well, to prepare the food with care, and even to serve it properly: one could be reduced to gnawing in one's bunk. The food itself too is important in this regard. I carried a variety of natural foodstuffs, like rice, dried meats, etc., which last almost for ever, and virtually no tins. I baked my own bread and, as an aid to gracious living, took 10 gallons of wine in polythene casks. The living must indeed have been too gracious for it only lasted half way.

"On 8th July in about 25½°N, 61°W this progress was halted by a disastrously prolonged period of calms which finally put paid to any chance I had of making a fast passage. It lasted until the 18th, although there were puffs and zephyrs, and a benevolent current kept me moving roughly towards my destination. But for the most part the seas were metallic, with no swell, and no noise except the groaning of the parrels round the mast. It was a time, as I noted, of almost interplanetary isolation. The sea surface in this lonely area was thick with primitive forms of life and sargasso weed floated in profusion. I had a curious feeling of insecurity. Could I drift round the periphery of this maritime desert for ever, like the weed?

"Of course eventually the wind came in, after a night of violent thunder-storms (the more alarming because I had no conductor.) But from then on I had a predominance of head winds and between 17th and 18th July actually moved backwards, set by a current running counter to the general direction. On the 22nd I entered the Gulf Stream, some 60 miles off Cape Hatteras, but by the next day I was once more becalmed, setting gently south-west in one of its meanders. My morale was now rather vulnerable: I had had enough. However, on the 24th a fresh south-westerly blew up and I had a beautiful run in the Gulf Stream, albeit in somewhat turbulent seas.

"That afternoon I ran out of the warm blue water into opaque seas; the Gulf Stream had turned east. By the 25th it was blowing about force 7 from the west with quite a heavy sea running. Off Cape Henry I smelt the sweet smell of land, and the first fly came aboard. (It puzzled me that it should be so far off-shore.) Then on the night of the 26th I saw the loom of Atlantic City and the following morning passed a fisherman's

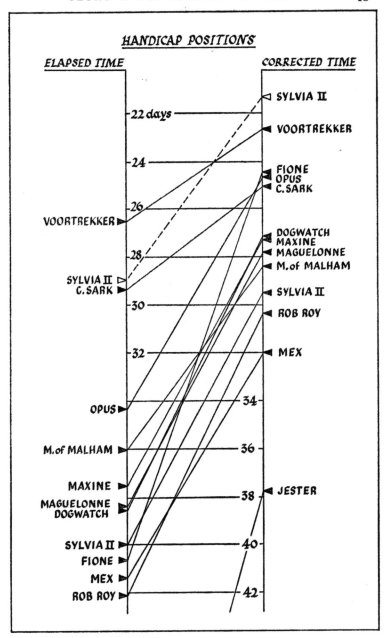

HANDICAP POSITIONS

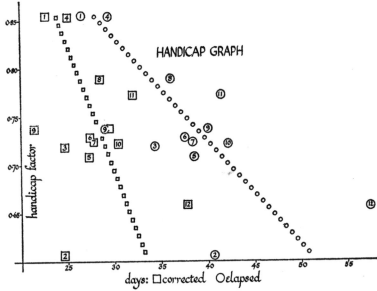

1. *Voortrekker* 2. *Fione* 3. *Opus* 4. *Spirit of Cutty Sark* 5. *Dogwatch* 6. *Maxime* 7. *Maguelonne* 8. *Myth of Malham* 9. *Sylvia II* 10. *Rob Roy* 11. *Mex* 12. *Jester*

dan buoy, a homely object that made me feel I had made the American continent. Finally, at dawn on the 28th, having sailed some 5,250 miles I made my landfall on Montauk Point at the eastern end of Long Island. After a lovely run up to Narragansset Bay I passed the finish, off Brenton Reef, 57 days 10 hours and 13 minutes out."

This ocean passage places the whole endeavour in context: more than merely a race to be won outright or by handicap, it is the crossing of an ocean which demands art in the navigation, stamina in the sailing and above all, integrity in the mind. Each man arriving at Newport has won his own race his own way. *Jester* qualified as a 'finisher' equally with the other boats that completed the race.

The application to this race of wordly standards of glory can seem incongruous to those taking part, for whom the criterion is the virtue inherent in each crossing, how one man in one boat accepts and uses whatever Providence provides. Any glory there may be is but a shadow of that virtue.

FINISHING LIST

Overall Placing	Yacht	Elapsed Time			Corrected Time			Handicap Placing
		days	hrs	mins	days	hrs	mins	
1	Sir Thomas Lipton	25	20	33				
2	Voortrekker	26	13	42	22	16	51	1
3	Cheers	27	00	13				
4	Spirit of Cutty Sark	29	10	17	25	02	44	4
5	Golden Cockerel	31	16	24				
6	Opus	34	08	23	24	16	14	3
7	Gancia Girl	34	13	15				
8	Myth of Malham	36	01	41	28	11	01	8
9	Maxine	37	13	47	27	08	36	6
10	Maguelonne	38	09	10	27	18	17	7
11	Dogwatch	38	12	13	27	06	20	5
12	Sylvia II	40	00	16	29	12	29	9
		(*29	00	16	21	10	27)	
13	Fione	40	14	13	24	14	22	2
14	Mex	41	10	46	32	00	04	11
15	Rob Roy	42	03	49	30	10	20	10
16	Startled Faun	45	10	08				
17	Amistad	47	18	05				
	Goodwin II	50	19	48	(disqualified)			
18	Jester	57	10	40	37	19	43	12

* Passage time after second start on 12th June

Retired *Pen Duick IV, Raph, San Giorgio, Coila, Yaksha, Ocean Highlander, Guntur III, Zeevalk, Koala III, Ambrima, La Delirante, White Ghost, Aye-Aye, Wileca, Atlantis III, Tamouré.*

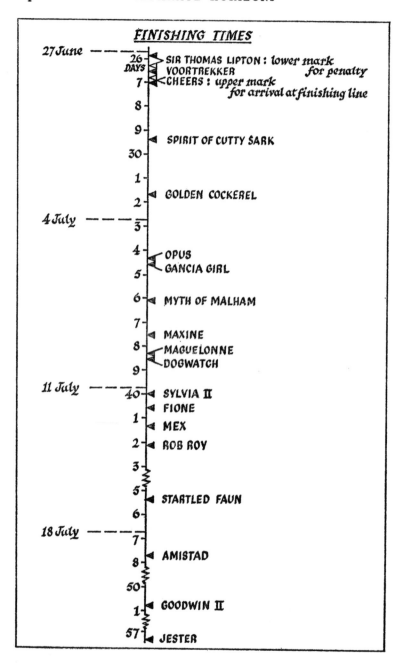

FINISHING TIMES

27 June

26 DAYS — SIR THOMAS LIPTON : *lower mark for penalty*
VOORTREKKER
7 — CHEERS : *upper mark for arrival at finishing line*

8

9 — SPIRIT OF CUTTY SARK
30

1
2 — GOLDEN COCKEREL

4 July

3

4 — OPUS
5 — GANCIA GIRL

6 — MYTH OF MALHAM

7
8 — MAXINE
— MAGUELONNE
9 — DOGWATCH

11 July

40 — SYLVIA II
— FIONE
1 — MEX
2 — ROB ROY

3
5 — STARTLED FAUN

6

18 July

7
8 — AMISTAD

50
1 — GOODWIN II

57 — JESTER

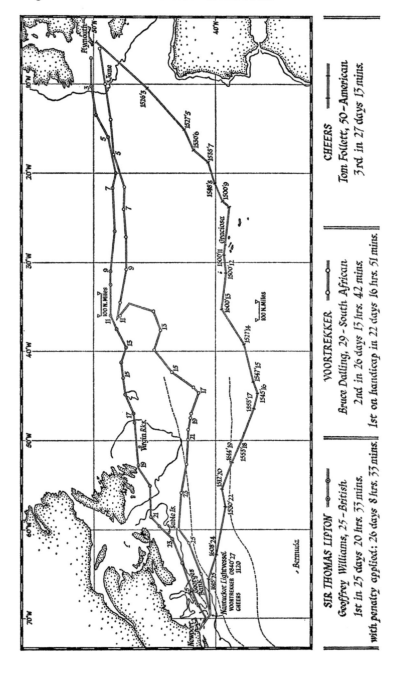

SIR THOMAS LIPTON

Geoffrey Williams, 25 – British.
1st in 25 days 20 hrs. 33 mins.
with penalty applied: 26 days 8 hrs. 33 mins.

VOORTREKKER

Bruce Dalling, 29 – South African.
2nd in 26 days 13 hrs. 42 mins.
1st on handicap in 22 days 16 hrs. 51 mins.

CHEERS

Tom Follett, 50 – American
3rd in 27 days 13 mins.

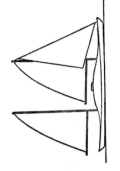

Cheers
proa (schooner)
double canoe, (development of
proa concept).
Dick Newick
Dick Newick, West Indies
1967
40'
36'
16.8'
4·3'
486 sq ft
1.24 tons

Voortrekker
ketch
monohull

E. G. Van de Stadt
Thesens, South Africa
1967
50'
39.6'
11.5'
8.5'
980 sq ft
6.5 tons

Sir Thomas Lipton
ketch
monohull

Robert Clark Ltd.
Derek Kelsall, England
1968
56.16'
42'
12'
8'
1,171 sq ft
12.25 tons

rig
hull

designer
builder
year
LOA
LWL
beam
draft
sail area
displacement

0 5 10 15 20 25 30

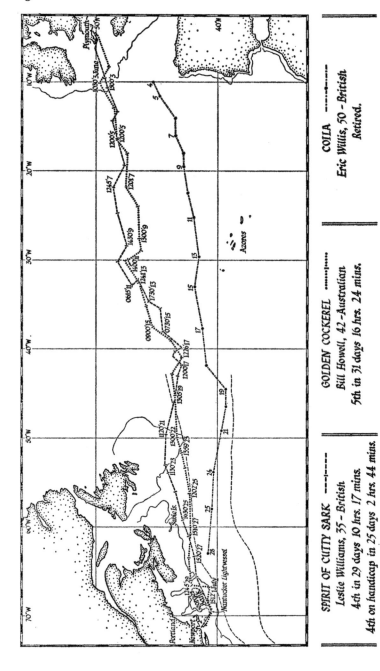

SPIRIT OF CUTTY SARK —·—·—
Leslie Williams, 35 – British
4th in 29 days 10 hrs. 17 mins.
4th on handicap in 25 days 2 hrs. 44 mins.

GOLDEN COCKEREL ·········
Bill Howell, 42 – Australian
5th in 31 days 16 hrs. 24 mins.

COILA —————
Eric Willis, 50 – British
Retired.

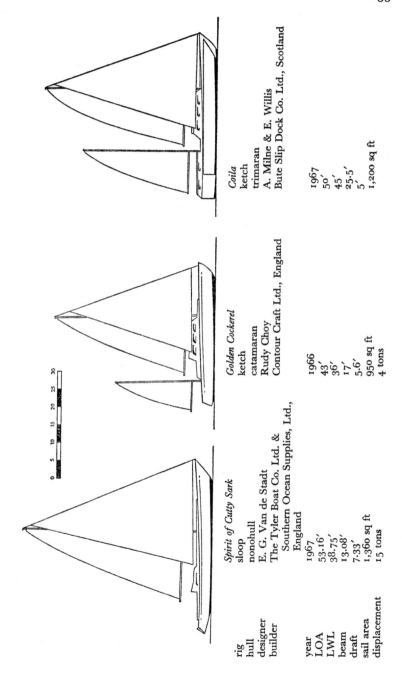

	Spirit of Cutty Sark	*Golden Cockerel*	*Coila*
rig	sloop	ketch	ketch
hull	nonohull	catamaran	trimaran
designer	E. G. Van de Stadt	Rudy Choy	A. Milne & E. Willis
builder	The Tyler Boat Co. Ltd. & Southern Ocean Supplies, Ltd., England	Contour Craft Ltd., England	Bute Slip Dock Co. Ltd., Scotland
year	1967	1966	1967
LOA	53.16'	43'	50'
LWL	38.75'	36'	45'
beam	13.08'	17'	25.5'
draft	7.33'	5.6'	5'
sail area	1,360 sq ft	950 sq ft	1,200 sq ft
displacement	15 tons	4 tons	

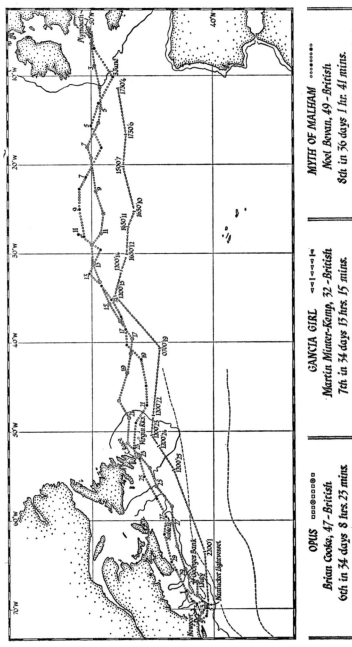

OPUS □□□◎◎◎◎◎◎
Brian Cooke, 47 – British
6th in 34 days 8 hrs. 25 mins.
3rd on handicap in 24 days 16 hrs. 14 mins.

GANCIA GIRL ◅◁◁◁◁◅
Martin Minter-Kemp, 32 – British
7th in 34 days 13 hrs. 15 mins.

MYTH OF MALHAM ◦◦◦◦◦◦◦●◦
Noel Bevan, 49 – British
8th in 36 days 1 hr. 41 mins.
8th on handicap in 28 days 11 hrs. 1 min.

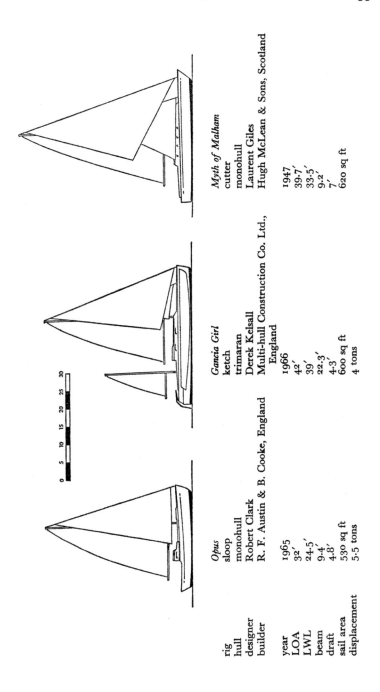

	Opus	*Gancia Girl*	*Myth of Malham*
rig	sloop	ketch	cutter
hull	monohull	trimaran	monohull
designer	Robert Clark	Derek Kelsall	Laurent Giles
builder	R. F. Austin & B. Cooke, England	Multi-hull Construction Co. Ltd., England	Hugh McLean & Sons, Scotland
year	1965	1966	1947
LOA	32′	42′	39·7′
LWL	24·5′	39′	33·5′
beam	9·4′	22·3′	9·2′
draft	4·8′	4·3′	7′
sail area	530 sq ft	600 sq ft	620 sq ft
displacement	5·5 tons	4 tons	

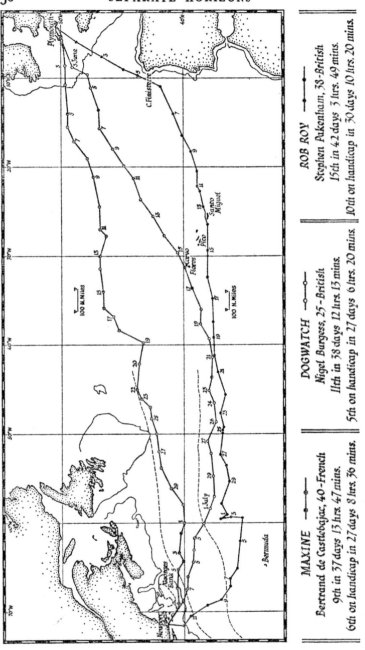

MAXINE —●—
Bertrand de Castlebajac, 40—French
9th in 37 days 13 hrs. 47 mins.
6th on handicap in 27 days 8 hrs. 36 mins.

DOGWATCH —○—
Nigel Burgess, 25—British
11th in 38 days 12 hrs. 13 mins.
5th on handicap in 27 days 6 hrs. 20 mins.

ROB ROY —●—
Stephen Pakenham, 38—British
15th in 42 days 3 hrs. 49 mins.
10th on handicap in 30 days 10 hrs. 20 mins.

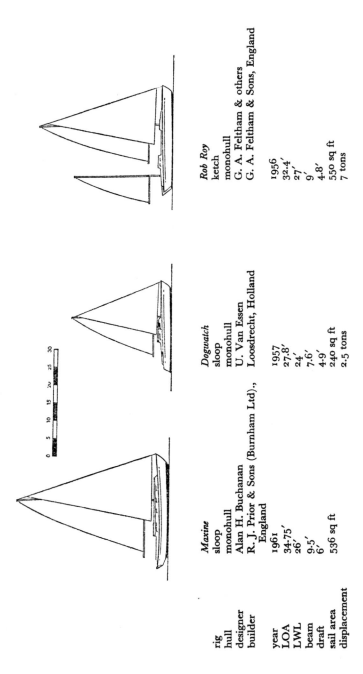

	Maxine	*Dogwatch*	*Rob Roy*
rig	sloop	sloop	ketch
hull	monohull	monohull	monohull
designer	Alan H. Buchanan	U. Van Essen	G. A. Feltham & others
builder	R. J. Prior & Sons (Burnham Ltd)., England	Loosdrecht, Holland	G. A. Feltham & Sons, England
year	1961	1957	1956
LOA	34·75'	27.8'	32.4'
LWL	26'	24'	27'
beam	9·5'	7.6'	9'
draft	6'	4.9'	4.8'
sail area	536 sq ft	240 sq ft	550 sq ft
displacement		2.5 tons	7 tons

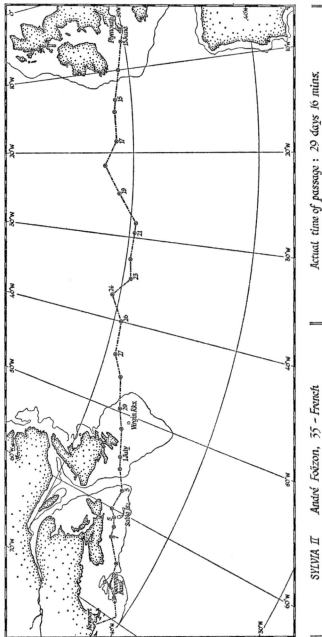

SYLVIA II   André Foëzon, 35 – French
12th in 40 days 16 mins.
9th on handicap in 29 days 12 hrs. 29 mins.

Actual time of passage : 29 days 16 mins.
which gives a record corrected time of
21 days 10 hrs. 27 mins.

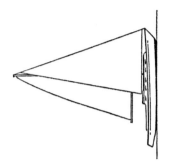

Sylvia II
rig   sloop
hull   monohull
designer   Sparkman & Stephens
LOA   36′

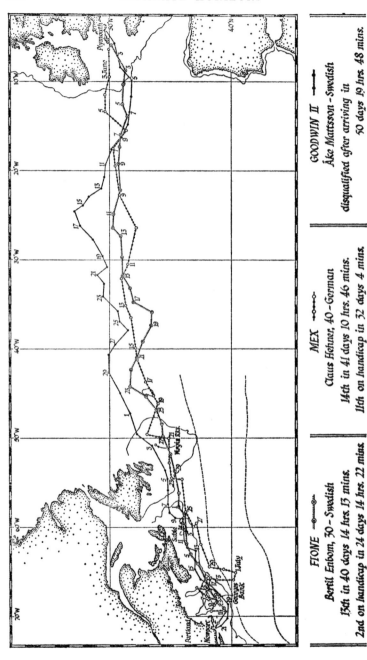

GOODWIN II •━━━━•
Åke Mattsson - Swedish
disqualified after arriving in
50 days 19 hrs. 48 mins.

MEX ◦━◦━◦━◦
Claus Hehner, 40 - German
14th in 41 days 10 hrs. 46 mins.
11th on handicap in 32 days 4 mins.

FIONE ◦━◦━◦━◦
Bertil Enbom, 30 - Swedish
15th in 40 days 14 hrs. 15 mins.
2nd on handicap in 24 days 14 hrs. 22 mins.

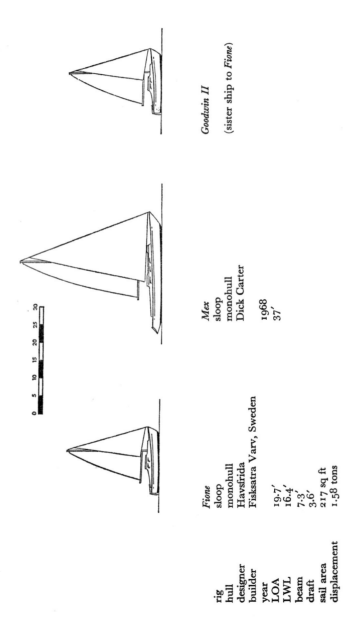

Fione
sloop
monohull
Havsfrida
Fisksatra Varv, Sweden

19.7'
16.4'
7.3'
3.6'
217 sq ft
1.58 tons

rig
hull
designer
builder
year
LOA
LWL
beam
draft
sail area
displacement

Mex
sloop
monohull
Dick Carter

1968
37'

Goodwin II

(sister ship to Fione)

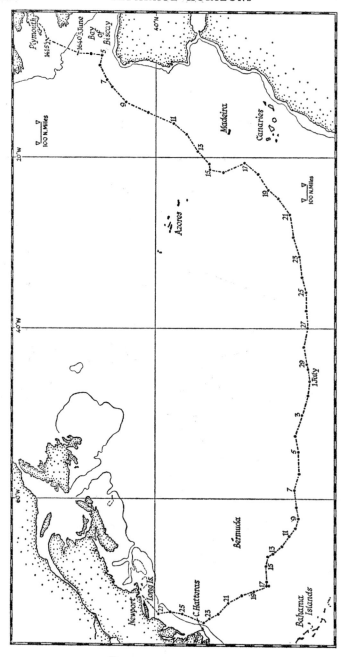

JESTER : Michael Richey, 50/51–British. 18th in 57 days 10 hrs. 40 mins. 12th on handicap in 37 days 19 hrs. 45 minutes.

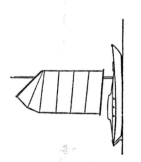

Jester

rig   chinese lug
hull   monohull
designer   H. G. Hasler
builder   Harry Feltham (Portsmouth) Ltd.,
           England

year   1953
LOA   25.9'
LWL   19.9'
beam   7.2'
draft   4'
sail area 248 sq ft

Appendix I Parallel logbook analysis I

Voortrekker Bruce Dalling	*Spirit of Cutty Sark* Leslie Williams	*Golden Cockerel* Bill Howell
9 June 1300 SW 5		
	1630 Storm jib: 10 rolls in main. 1730 A few vicious squalls now. 1930 Shook out 6 rolls– set working jib. 2200 W 6	2100 Gusting force 8
10 June 0700 W 7 0800 W 8	0200 W 6–7	
	0900 W 8 1000 W 7–8	1000 Line squall gusting force 10
	1200 W 8	
	1500 W 7–8 1700 W 6–7	**10 hours "hove to or almost"**
1800 W 5	1800 W 5–6 1900 SSW 5	1830 Force 6 + 2030 Sailing again
2200 S 4	2200 SE 7–8 2300 SE 8	2215 SW 5 2245 Line squalls
11 June 0200 E 4	0100 SE 9 Lowered main	0100 Force 10 **ahull**
	0400 SE 8–9	
0500 W 8 0600 W 10 **Lying ahull**	0515 Force 12	
	0700 Force 10–11 **ahull**	**34 hours**
1000 W 10–11 **13 hours**		1200 Force 7–8
	29 hours	
by 1900 Sailing again– force 8		1900 Sea worse, gusting force 9
2200 W 7 *12 June*		2200 Force 6
	1030 Sailing again	1100 Sailing again

Opus Brian Cooke	*Gancia Girl* Martin Minter-Kemp	*Myth of Malham* Noel Bevan
2400 Force 8		2400 SSW 7 +
0200 **"Virtually hove to"**		**"Partially hove to"**
5 hours		0500 **Hove to**
0700 Sailing again		**14 hours**
0900 Force 8		
		1230 W 6– sailing again
1500 "Lovely sunny afternoon" SW 3–4		1600 WSW 7
Overnight, wind increasing to gale from SSE.	0200 **ahull**	0200 SSW 8
		0400 Force 9 +
		0700 Force 10
		0730 **ahull**
0930 Main lowered		
1000 Force 9	**approx 26 hours**	**12 hours**
1100 Force 8		
1315 Force 9		
1430 Knock down		
21 hours main lowered		
1930 SSW 7–8		1900 Force 7— sailing again
2115 SW 6–8		
2230 Force 5	by dawn– sailing again	
0030 NNW 6		
0615 Hoisted main		

Parallel logbook analysis II

Cheers Tom Follett	Dogwatch Nigel Burgess	Rob Roy Stephen Pakenham
10 June 0130 Rain 0415 WSW 5 0530 WNW 7		 0600 NW 2
0730 WNW 6, sunshine rough sea		0730 W 3
	1200 Rain	"day and night of fair winds
1400 WNW 4		and angry squalls
1630 Sky clear	1630 Wind veered through 180°	with
1900 W 2		much
2300 WSW 4	2110 Pleasant evening NW	sail changing"
11 June	0200 Speed 1 knot– becoming calm	
0320 SW 5		0600 NW 1
0540 SSW 7–8 Rough sea		
0700 Overcast moving in		
		1115 Calm
1200 SSW 6 Rough sea	1345 Going well. A lovely day.	
1445 SSW 5 1515 Overcast moving in again		
1800 SSW 4	1800 3 knots–sea increasing	**becalmed 21 hours**
1950 No wind and lumpy sea 2030 Doused all sail Waiting for wind 2130 Breeze from SW		
12 June 0200 Doused all sail again 0430 Breeze from SSE 0500 SSE 5. Rain 0615 Force 8	0305 SSW 2	
0800 force 0-6 SSE to SSW 1000 SSE 8	0700 Big black cloud ahead	0715 SSE light air.

Cheers cont'd.	*Dogwatch* cont'd.	*Rob Roy* cont'd.
1025 Sudden wind shift to N in heavy rain Doused sail.		
1050 NE		
8 hours ahull		SSE 0–2 during day
1400 NNE 10		
1830 NE 8 Foresail up		
2230 Moderating	2110 Heard that Leslie Williams in force 12 wind.	
13 June 0430 NNW 5 Clear sky		
		0600 SSE 1 0630 S 2
	No entries in log from 2110/12th to 1200/15th	1030 S 3
		1200 S 3–4
		1430 SSW 4
		1800 SSW 2
1930 Best sail of the trip today. Reaching along in a steady force 5.		1930 Calm
		2100 NNW 6 +
14 June 0100 Wind moderating		
0630 NNW 4		0600 NNW 5
		1000 NNW 7–8 Reduced to working jib only

Parallel logbook analysis III

Cheers Tom Follett	*Voortrekker* Bruce Dalling
25 June	0900 It's bitter cold again.
0920 Mizzen off. Wind gusting force 8. Water temperature feels like Gulf Stream–can it be?	
0955 Mizzen up again.	1100 SSW force 3.
1110 Mizzen off. Another hard day at the office!	
1150 Wind SW force 8. Rain–overcast–sea rough.	
1315 Mizzen up.	1400 Visibility 200 yards.
	1500 About onto starboard tack. Very nasty sea running–the overfall and popple are taking 2 knots off our speed–just stops her dead in her tracks.
1600 Wind veering and gusty. Fog.	
1750 Came onto starboard tack. Thick fog. Wind WNW force 4	1800 Wind force 3.
	1900 Visibility 50 yards.
2000 Fog lifting	2000 The wind is all over the place in both strength and direction. Result–nil progress. I feel bloody miserable quite honestly.
2025 Rain	
2130 Flat calm	
2145 A breeze. Rain squalls.	
2155 Heavy rain.	
2245 Flat calm. Sails off to await developments. Thunder showers.	
26 June	
	0100 I've never known frustration like this voyage in my life before.
0330 Light easterly breeze–underway.	Got 1 hour's sleep during the night–we spent the whole night just going round in circles.
0345 Set No. 2 jib. Very light breeze. Rain.	
0445 Came onto port tack	0400 Becalmed

(To illustrate contrast and a little correlation)

Cheers cont'd.	*Voortrekker* cont'd.

0630 25 days from Plymouth and back on starboard tack.

0630 Rather a complicated weather system. Forecast from Boston calls for easterly winds to force 8.

0700 Gale warning from Boston.
0800 Gale warning from Cape Cod.

0830 Port tack.
0845 Doused jib. Doing no good unless we go too far off course. Not enough wind to warrant that.

0900 Visibility 300 yards.

0940 Breeze piping up. Will it last?
0950 No! fluky wind. All sails off until it settles down. Looks like I am trapped here 135 miles from Nantucket Light.

1100 Sails up again. On port tack. Wind aft.
1140 Starboard tack. Wind ENE force 4.
1200 Mizzen off–unable to hold course with both sails.
1245 Steady breeze at last. ENE force 4–5. Rain.

1400 Wind E force 3.

1415 ENE force 4. Fog
1445 Set mizzen again. Wind a bit more in the north and rather light.

1640 Thick fog–no wind. Oh, joy!
1700 Wind shifting. When will it end? SSW now.
1710 Close-hauled on port tack– wind SW

1700 A most peculiar thing just happened. The wind from NE dropped suddenly, and a vicious squall came through from the W. The sea just stood on end, not knowing what had happened, with spray everywhere.

1835 Here we go again! On starboard tack; wind NW.

1930 Very lumpy seas tossing us about. Still, we make a little progress on course to the lightship. What dreary weather! Worse than England. Never seen such fluky winds as we've been having today.

Parallel log book analysis III *(cont'd.)*

Cheers cont'd.

2000 Wind N force 3-4. Heavy
    swell rolling in from SW plus
    other swells from here and
    there. A very rough ride even
    though off the wind.
2130 Port tack.
2145 All sail off. No wind. Lumps in
    the ocean.

2400 Hoisted foresail to see how it
    goes. Light easterly breeze.

27 June
0100 A passable breeze.

0300 ENE force 5. Fairly heavy sea.
    Running under foresail only.
    Temperature cold.

0500 ENE force 6. Heavy seas.

0600 From Plymouth 26 days.
0645 Reefed both sails and set
    the foresail. N force 8.
    Visibility rather poor in light
    fog.

1035 Doused foresail in strong wind.
1115 Foresail up.
1120 Nantucket Lightvessel abeam.

Voortrekker cont'd.

2000 Gusting force 7.

2400 Wind force 5-7.

0400 Visibility ± 500 yards. Raining.

0500 NNE force 3-5. I was very
    fortunate last night–the wind
    moderated and held steady and I
    was able to get 6 hours sleep.
    It was a very heavy
    uncomfortable ride, mind you,
    as the sea is very lumpy.

0700 Blowing the clappers again–
    ENE force 6-7.

0840 Rounded Nantucket Lightvessel.

Ideas on routes are rightly developed from the experience of each race; I find two aspects of 1968 thought provoking.

1. The passage of *Cheers*. Whether Tom Follett intended it or not, he has introduced a new style to the race. In the past, we have found it natural to plan for the race by drawing several likely lines across a chart from Plymouth to Newport and then analyse, so far as patience takes us, the relative merits of the routes which those lines represent. Careful study of average winds and current, etc., set against the distance, leads to selecting what seems the best line across the chart.

And to follow it we then try; but, particularly on the direct route, the wind will blow us this way and that, and in all honesty the actual tracks by which we cross may bear very little resemblance to the neat theory of the planned lines! Nevertheless, the ideal of following an orderly line across the ocean has largely held sway until the passage of *Cheers*.

Tom Follett talks about 'routes' but not 'lines' or 'turning points' — "I spent a good bit of time on Pilot charts before I came to England and I picked out a couple of routes that I would like to take. There were two things which decided me on the final route: one was the long range forecast the night before the race which showed the ice going down as far as 45°N (I did not particularly want to get mixed up in that!) and showing head winds on the northerly route; and then the second thing that made up my mind was what the wind was actually doing when I took off — it was west-north-west.

"I did not really plan to go as far south as I did. I thought I would keep her close reaching on the starboard tack, heading off in a general south-westerly direction, hoping that I would not go any further south than 39°N, and then bend back up and miss the northern part of the Azores by a hundred miles or so. As it was, I went about 20 miles south of Flores and then kept on going all the way down to the 36th parallel!"

By convention, this approach to the race sounds far too loose and 'free-ranging'. Yet as Tom reached the 36th parallel he was abreast *Voortrekker* and *Sir Thomas Lipton*, and about to take the lead. (A glance at the relative sizes of the three boats on page 148 will give a reminder, if needed, of what an achievement this was.)

For the direct route, had Tom plotted a 'turning point' south of the Virgin Rocks? "Not really; what I planned to do with this boat was to take off and always keep her close reaching. By looking at the Pilot charts and reading what goes on in the North Atlantic (also partly from my own experience when delivering yachts) I was convinced that if you get the wind setting you south one day, then the next two or three days you get it setting north — I planned to keep the boat close reaching all the time."

In following the Azores route, how had he planned to cross the Gulf Stream? "The Gulf Stream didn't worry me too much. What I planned to do was to take a straight shot right across, if possible, as soon as I got in

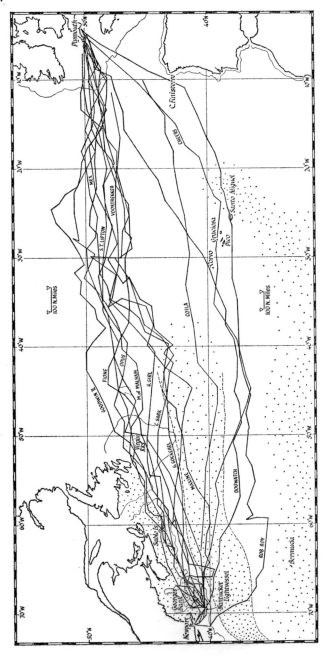

Agglomeration of tracks with dots to show awkward areas

it . . . I never tacked in an attempt to get to any definite point. I tacked a few times because of fluky winds, but never with any idea in mind of heading for a particular point in the ocean."

If this seems suggestive for multihulls in general and the Azores route in particular, does it affect our outlook on monohulls beating into the prevailing wind on the direct route?

The line of the great circle route may seem artificial *if* the usual head-winds materialise, and anyway, as mentioned in Chapter 3, the single great circle line from the Bishop Rock Lighthouse to the Nantucket Light-vessel passes some 20 miles inland across Newfoundland: one is in fact drawing two great circle lines either side of a turning point. It is artificial to draw the two lines precisely to and from Cape Race — it will almost certainly be left a respectful distance to starboard. If more than a few miles of clearance is allowed for because of the likelihood of fog, the second great circle leg becomes entangled too closely with Sable Island! If a ruler is placed on the gnomonic chart and swung round in an arc on the Nantucket Lightvessel until it gives a line that clears Sable Island to the south, one can draw a second leg that passes well south of the Virgin Rocks and also St George's Bank. It looks seamanlike and is in fact the route drawn in the Admiralty *Ocean Passages for the World* (marked 'seldom possible'!); it is taking one roughly along the middle of the direct route *but* it is sadly south of that romantic great circle! The idea of the 'middle line' is developed in the next point.

2. Avoiding the awkward areas. From the beginning it has been obvious that the Gulf Stream should be left well alone, except for the crossing of it made on the Azores route. It has also been clear that the Azores route passes somewhat closely north of a large area of high pressure. What has not been so clear is the probable lack of wind between Cape Race and the Nantucket Lightvessel.

Before the 1968 race I made calculations through both the U.S. Pilot Chart and the Met. Office equivalent, to compare the theoretical total of calms, light and variable winds on the direct route and the Azores route. To my astonishment, both charts suggested 1 per cent more likelihood of calms, light and variable winds on the direct route. Calculations like this may seem to be far removed from actual sailing, but it highlighted to me the risk of losing the wind between Cape Race and the Nantucket Light-vessel. In practical terms, what has happened in the race seems to have produced a rule of thumb: one should not sail between Sable Island and Nova Scotia. Several men have sailed in deliberately and got away with it. Others were already close to the area when the wind headed them in, and they do not wish to repeat the experience!

If this rule of thumb is accepted, both routes are flanked by awkward areas once they are abreast the Gulf Stream, and in terms of being pushed about by the wind, perhaps the theoretical line of each route should pass along the middle between the awkward areas; or perhaps the whole idea of theoretical lines begins to crumble! Certainly I feel this: we have tended to concentrate too much on the lines and too little on the awkward areas. It is surely less important, in practice, to be calculating how far one has diverged from a line than to be watching how nearly one is approaching an awkward area. Steamship routes are drawn as lines, and the old sailing ship routes more generally as broad bands of varying width.

In conclusion, it seems altogether right in the planning stage to draw the lines across the chart and calculate the average winds and current etc. If the winds are free the lines can then be followed. But in normal conditions it does seem appropriate to sail with a certain freedom, using the given winds to best advantage, concentrating on avoiding the awkward areas rather than on trying to follow a predetermined line across the chart.

"I was up every hour, on the hour, from leaving Plymouth to arriving at Newport" — Brian Cooke.

How does the singlehander race his boat continuously day and night? The wind can do three things while he is asleep: blow up to make him awkwardly overcanvassed; drop so that he is no longer racing efficiently; or haul round, taking him off course. There is also the important problem of meeting other vessels and icebergs.

Each man develops a system for trying to get the best out of himself. Brian Cooke was "up every hour, to make sure that the boat was going in the right direction, going at the best possible speed, and the self-steering gear and other essential parts of the boat functioning properly. So my sleep was in short snatches . . . total per day was on average 4 hours." This system achieved third place on handicap.

For his second place on handicap, Bertil Enbom slept for only 20–30 minutes at a stretch, waking to a kitchen pinger clock, but his total was about 7 hours a day.

One might think that the greater daily total for Bertil was significant, but for first on handicap Bruce Dalling averaged only 3½–4 hours each day, using a pinger clock set 30 minutes ahead each time he went down to rest.

The three of them had one thing in common: they were leaving the boat to sail itself for short intervals only, using an alarm clock to achieve this. To be up every hour, on the hour, gives much less than an hour's sleep at a stretch, and Brian's periods of sleep may have been little different to those of Bruce and Bertil.

This 'short interval' system gains in plausibility in being followed by Geoffrey Williams as outright winner and André Foëzon as holding the record time on handicap. (André had two pinger clocks but became so exhausted by his sheer determination that in the end he was liable to sleep through both!)

The painful use of pinger clocks might therefore seem obligatory for serious racing, but the multihulls were not, of course, handicapped; Tom Follett and Bill Howell–two fine seamen who raced superbly–used a different system. Tom Follett: "I've never used an alarm clock. I slept very lightly, and the least little thing that happened, I was awake and looking around." He normally slept for 1–1½ hours at a stretch, totalling daily 6–8 hours — "plenty of sleep!" Bill Howell likes to have "a relaxed night from about midnight to 0800 if the weather is alright." But in this particular race he only had "a very broken type of sleep" (Bill does use an alarm clock when it seems appropriate.)

It would be very convenient if everyone could be classified into one of two groups. The first group would use an alarm clock to wake after some 30 minutes of sleep; it would total under 5 hours each day, and the men would become progressively more tired during the race. The second group would sleep for widely varying periods, depending on conditions, reckoning that an awareness was maintained during sleep so that one would wake 'on demand'. This group would normally sleep for more than 5 hours each day and should not become more tired during the race.

If the 1 hour interval is taken as giving the essential division in mental approach, then one can separate those in the 1968 race roughly into two halves on either side, remembering, of course, that the 'on demand' men may only sleep for a few minutes at a time when conditions are difficult. However, the total for each day and the use of alarm clocks refuses to be neatly classified. For instance, Leslie Williams normally slept for 30 minutes at a time, but day or night "if I was not doing anything I slept," and he totalled up to 10 hours each day. Also, Nigel Burgess and I slept much the same periods, averaging 1½ hours, towards much the same total (5–6 hours), but whereas I never set an alarm clock during the race, Nigel always did, generally waking about 30 minutes before it rang. We were both basically on demand, but cannot claim the awareness of Jean Yves Terlain — "when I sleep I feel the boat always."

This 'awareness' is an important aspect of sleep. It could only be expected that the 'short interval' men would tend to become progressively less aware of what their boats were doing while they were asleep, contrasting with Tom Follett — "one thing which wakes me up very quickly is any change in motion." This degree of sensitivity is unusual, and most on demand men would not deny their liability, when called, to remain firmly 'off!'

What about premonition, that intriguing awareness to danger or change in weather before the normal senses of the mind can detect them? Tom: "I don't know. I often wake up 'like that', and now and then there will be nothing going on, but again there will be — I think it's just the odd feeling." Despite his scepticism, I find it interesting that he was awake on each occasion when his boat needed him: he does seem very much at home on the sea.

Martin Minter-Kemp is more specific: "Premonition to danger does exist–for instance, the cap shroud (the starboard outer cap shroud parted to one strand about 12 feet from the deck)–I was just about to turn in and I had a feeling that something wasn't — well, not even a feeling, I just went and had a look and there it was." Martin, as well as Leslie Williams, took avoiding action on the feeling that an iceberg lay ahead, but neither will ever know if one was there!

It is empirical that premonition is more likely to come to those who sleep well towards a good total each day, but I must add that if half-a-dozen of us believed in it, as many denied its existence!

It might be tempting to conclude that the on demand system is more seamanlike and the short interval one more efficient for racing, but I would not suggest that the short interval men are lacking as seamen, nor the on demand men poor at racing!

No two men followed exactly the same pattern of sleep. This seems altogether right, and one can conclude that each man should find what is natural to him and develop that, rather than attempt to conform to any particular system which looks superior.

I qualified with the help of Southampton Technical College as Radio-telegraph operator in order to operate as a "full radiotelegraph ship."

Two transmitters were specially designed, and had type approval just for the duration of the race. These were both transistorised, 40 watts H/F (8 MC) and 75 watts (500 KC), each transmitter being of very high efficiency and only weighing 2 pounds. Over a year was spent in close liason with the GPO during the design and acceptance of these transmitters. No trouble was experienced with their operation, and many messages were sent and received. Most of *Myth of Malham's* messages were encoded, mainly to save money since the minimum charge is 1s. 8d. per word.

The main aerial was the two standing backstays in parallel, the auxiliary aerial being taped up the shrouds, enabling duplex Radiotelegraph operation.

Receivers: 1 H/F Quick Search (GPO R/T Meetings Monitor); 1 H/F for Radiotelegraph; 1 all-wave for Broadcast, 2,182 Monitoring etc; 1 VLF for Rugby, Washington and Loran using computed half convergency lines specially plotted as overlays by Elliott 920 computer; special D/F facilities VLF, L/F, and 2,182; 1,500 KC receiver (modified Brookes and Gatehouse Homer), also a directional radar receiver.

Camper and Nicholsons very kindly lent a H/F receiver, which performed admirably. Apart from Hecta and Harrier, *Myth of Malham* carried a home-made anemometer wind direction/course indicator made from surplus aircraft instruments. The batteries were charged by a thermoelectric generator from the Taylor cabin heater.

The sensitive water thermometer had a sensor element in the keel, and was capable of detecting a change of 1/50th of a degree centigrade. It was invaluable in mid-Atlantic for a latitude change check, 10 miles being easily recognised as a relative change. Full Met. Office North Atlantic isotherm information was carried. Her off-course alarm contains no magnetic compass, and has the advantage of increasing noise with increasing course deviation.

The two Philips tape recorders also enabled a great deal of data on instru-ment recordings and readings to be logged for future reference.

All this electronics worked well, the only failure being the omni radar aerial, the lead of which was broken when one of the spreaders came adrift in mid-Atlantic.

Myth of Malham also had a specially modified mechanical calculator for sight reduction, and carried a quartz chronometer lent by Golay of Switzerland.

I certainly slept soundly and well, knowing that the alarms would do their stuff. Even the alarm clock was electric, bolted up on the opposite side of the boat to ensure a quick hop out of the berth to stifle it. It enabled one to wake up, in some cases just before it went off, for it had a bell on the threshold of pain!

The one thing which I did not have was a set level on the anemometer

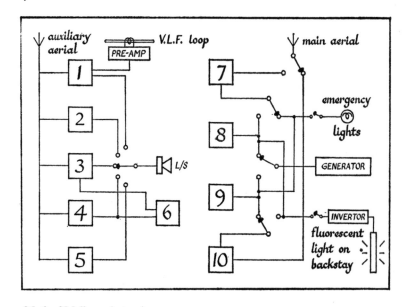

Myth of Malham electronics
Equipment using self-contained batteries:—
1. V.L.F. Receiver; 10–110 Kc/s
2. 500 Kc/s Receiver (modified Brookes and Gatehouse)
3. All wave Receiver
4. H.F. Quick Search Receiver; 8–16 Mc/s
5. H.F. Receiver for radiotelegraphy; 2–30 Mc/s
6. Two Philips tape recorders
Equipment using 36 volt batteries:—
7. 40 Watt H.F. transistor transmitter
8. Main
9. Emergency
10. 75 Watt L.F. transistor transmitter

so that when it started to revolve it would trigger off a buzzer (alternatively, if you wanted warning that the wind was increasing, you could set it so that if it went above, for instance, force 6 it would trigger off an alarm.)

As I did not have this, I kept the ghoster up and took the sheet down through the forehatch and tied it to my ankle in the berth. It worked very well, and I would highly recommend it to anybody who wants to sleep in a calm and not miss any wind.

Appendix V Select Bibliography

Singlehanded crossings of the North Atlantic 1866–1968

Introductory: small boat crossings up to, and including, the 1960 race:—
Humphrey Barton–*Atlantic Adventurers* (Adlard Coles Ltd.)

Author	Yacht	Title and Publisher
1960 race		
David Lewis	*Cardinal Vertue*	*The Ship Would Not Travel Due West* (Temple Press Ltd.)
Francis Chichester	*Gypsy Moth III*	*Alone Across the Atlantic* (GeorgeAllen&UnwinLtd.)
Val Howells	*Eira*	*Sailing into Solitude* (Temple Press Books, London)
1964 race		
Eric Tabarly	*Pen Duick II*	*Lonely Victory* (Souvenir Press)
J. R. L. Anderson		*The Greatest Race in the World* (Hodder & Stoughton)
1968 race		
Bertrand de Castelbajac	*Maxine*	*de Plymouth à Newport, par le sud de Nantucket* (La Table Ronde)
John Groser		*Atlantic Venture* (Ward Lock & Co. Ltd.)
Alain Gliksman	*Raph*	*Les Solitaires de l'Atlantique* (Editions Maritimes d'Outre Mer)
Tom Follett, Dick Newick and Jim Morris	*Cheers*	*Project Cheers* (Adlard Coles Ltd.)
Geoffrey Williams	*Sir Thomas Lipton*	*Sir Thomas Lipton Wins* (Peter Davies)
Åke Mattsson	*Goodwin II*	*Vogspel* (Rabén & Sjögren)
Edith Baumann	*Koala III*	*Seule Vingt-cinq Jours Contre l'Atlantique* (Flammarion, Paris)

Appendix VI

Beaufort Number	Limits of Wind Speed in knots (measured at a height of 33 feet above sea level)	Descriptive Term	Sea Criterion
0	Less than 1	**Calm**	Sea like a mirror.
1	1—3	**Light air**	Ripples with the appearance of scales are formed but without foam crests.
2	4—6	**Light breeze**	Small wavelets, still short but more pronounced. Crests have a glassy appearance and do not break.
3	7—10	**Gentle breeze**	Large wavelets. Crests begin to break. Foam of glassy appearance. Perhaps scattered white horses.
4	11—16	**Moderate breeze**	Small waves, becoming longer; fairly frequent white horses.
5	17—21	**Fresh breeze**	Moderate waves, taking a more pronounced long form; many white horses are formed (Chance of some spray).
6	22—27	**Strong breeze**	Large waves begin to form; the white foam crests are more extensive everywhere (Probably some spray).
7	28—33	**Near gale**	Sea heaps up and white foam from breaking waves begins to be blown in streaks along the direction of the wind.
8	34—40	**Gale**	Moderately high waves of greater length; edges of crests

			begin to break into spindrift. The foam is blown in well-marked streaks along the direction of the wind.
9	41—47	**Strong gale**	High waves. Dense streaks of foam along the direction of the wind. Crests of waves begin to topple, tumble and roll over. Spray may affect visibility.
10	48—55	**Storm**	Very high waves with long overhanging crests. The resulting foam in great patches is blown in dense white streaks along the direction of the wind. On the whole the surface of the sea takes a white appearance. The tumbling of the sea becomes heavy and shock-like. Visibility affected.
11	56—63	**Violent storm**	Exceptionally high waves. (Small and medium-sized ships might be for a time lost to view behind the waves). The sea is completely covered with long white patches of foam lying along the direction of the wind. Everywhere the edges of the wave crests are blown into froth. Visibility affected.
12	64 +	**Hurricane**	The air is filled with foam and spray. Sea completely white with driving spray; visibility very seriously affected.

Index